.

A SLICE OF LIFE AT SEA

George W. Robinson

First published in 2017 by
Moira Brown
Broughty Ferry
Dundee. DD5 2HZ
www.publishkindlebooks4u.co.uk

ISBN13: 978 1 52147 165 4

1920 to 1924

In the North Country town of Gateshead, on the River Tyne, I was the only son, then ten years of age, of a family comprising Mother, four sisters and myself. My father had died two years previously, leaving behind him a moderate butchering business to be attended to by the family.

The ambition of the entire Robinson family, with the exception of myself, was to see the then rather diminutive heir follow in the usual footsteps; my future being all planned out for me by my four sisters, leaving my ambitions and intentions, if any in those early days, a mere voice in the wilderness.

Today one very seldom sees the butcher's boy with his basket on his hip delivering the meat. Possibly in this way we have improved with the times, for I am quite certain there was no bigger basket than the one I had to carry. Customers possibly get their meat on time now, for dogfights, a game of marbles or even a seat and one of the "penny dreadfuls", were all natural obstacles between my leaving the shop and delivering the goods.

One incident regarding delivery stands out in my mind. I was sent to some kennels with a parcel of meat for the purpose of feeding dogs over the weekend. The day being a Saturday there was the usual matinee at the local cinema. Pearl White had been left hanging over a cliff by her shoelaces the week before and I was rather anxious to see if they were still holding out. When I arrived at the kennels I could get no reply from the front of the house so I made my way to the back. Time was short, and Pearl was still hanging over that cliff! Even with the noise of the dogs barking, added to that of my kicking the door, there was still no reply. So over the wall went the dog meat and off to the matinee went George. Sunday duly arrived, also the owner of the dogs, all of them ill (the dogs, not the owner). I had thrown approximately one stone of raw meat right into the kennels amongst the dogs - did they have a day out that Saturday!

During the years of my job of being errand boy, I believe my salary was a trip to the pictures occasionally and my tips - they were most welcome. One part of my work was to go to Newcastle Meat Market, usually on Tuesday morning, for meat. There were probably lots of people who, watching a small boy with the carcass of a sheep on a barrow crossing the bridge, must have thought I had stolen it. I'm quite sure at the time I would have been very pleased to have had it stolen from me.

In addition to the ordinary day-school, there were choir practices at St. Columba's church and services three times on Sunday for I which received what to me then was the wonderful sum of four shillings per quarter. Have you, the reader, ever worn one of those so-called collars that choirboys had to wear? If so, you can believe me when I say I did not have to live to 1950 to know what controls were!

Upon every chance that offered itself I would slip away to the quayside at Newcastle to look at the ships. They were wonderful to me. What visions a boy's mind can conjure up. Books of every description, even the daily papers, were all read with relish should they have an article on the sea. I had previously heard talk about AB's or able-bodied seamen. That was the life for me. One day presenting myself aboard the S/S *Highlander*, at the age of thirteen years, and asking for an AB's job, I was returned to the quayside very quickly, wondering no doubt what was the language mates used in addition to English!

Nevertheless, at the age of fourteen, I was apprenticed to the shipping firm of W. A. Souter & Co., the Sheaf Steam Shipping Co. I was taken by my mother for the first interview and at the office desk a gentleman, who is still with the firm today, asked my mother why she had not brought me along. The reply was that she had, but I was so small, he could not see me for the desk. Captain Clarke, the marine superintendent, upon sighting me, immediately told me to grow up and return next year when I was somewhat larger. My hopes crashed completely. Then the unexpected happened. Captain Clarke stood up. Never to this day have I known whether it was being through a butcher's boy or a choir boy, I only know that I could speak up for myself when necessary. As Captain Clarke stood up, I said:

"Excuse me, Sir, are you a captain?"
"Yes, I am, young man."
"Then, sir, you are not very tall yourself, and I'm only starting!"

After a damn good shaking from my mother, I was signed up for four years. Before joining the ship I had to undergo the Board of Trade eyesight text. This consisted of reading letters from a card at a distance, also reading the colour of lights reflected in a mirror in a darkened room. After having successfully passed the card test, I was taken into the next room and placed alongside the lantern facing a large mirror on the opposite wall. The examiner put out all the room lights and asked me to name the colours from left to right that I could see in the mirror. I could not see any! After some debate as to why I could not see the very large sample lights showing in the mirror, the lights were again put on in the room and it was discovered that I was so small I could not even see in the mirror! This time with the help of some old ledgers placed upon the floor, yours truly parked on top of them, I passed my first board of Trade examination, with many more ahead of me!

1924

December 1924 saw me all fitted out in a double-breasted uniform, brass buttons too. I am sure there were not enough shop windows in Newcastle for me to pass and look at the reflection of all my four feet three inches! My mother even went to the length of having my photograph taken. It is still in existence but only comes to light when my wife decides to shift the furniture around again.

One large kit bag of clothing was hurriedly put together. When I look back at that bag I am amused at the amount of clothing I took with me. Mother possibly had the idea I was off for about two weeks. That voyage lasted almost two years. One shirt, one collar, one bar of Sunlight soap and one brand new uniform cap complete with badge.

On the 4th of December 1924, I was ordered to join the S/S *Sheaf Spear* then loading at Dunston Staithes. We were to carry a cargo of coal for Marseilles, France, and, in company with another new apprentice, William Hay of South Shields, I boarded my first ship. The Sheaf Spear was a standard ship built during the 1914-1918 war, 5100 tons deadweight. To me that day she looked the biggest ship I have ever seen, but I soon found out she had very limited accommodation and very scanty food.

By this time the ship was completely loaded and was lying off the buoys awaiting the tide. To get on deck from the Staithes one had to go across in a small sculler boat, with bags and baggage, then up the rope ladder on to the deck. Arriving on deck, we were told where our room was situated and then introduced to the Senior Apprentice, William Gee of Newcastle.

For the benefit of present day cadets and apprentices I will try to paint a picture of the half-deck. The room, on the after end of the bridge deck, comprised three bunks, one settee (wood, no cushions) and one food locker. Inside the locker there was very little food but thousands of cockroaches, of all colours, sizes and shapes. This then was to be our home for the next four years. Work, sleep, eat and bathe all in the one room, for the salary of sixty pounds for four years, plus a five-pound bonus if you stuck it to the end.

After having deposited our bags and "donkeys' breakfasts" (we also had to supply our own bedding), Billy Gee took us to meet the Chief Officer. Never shall I forget that day! Mr. Grisewood, the first Mate, was a real old shellback, from the days of sail. He took one look at Billy Hay and myself, remarking on our pretty uniforms and then told us to change into overalls or dungarees and return to him as soon as this had been done. He was sure he could find us something to do! Throughout the time I served under Mr. Grisewood I never knew him to be at a loss to find us something to do!

When we returned, dressed for work, we were presented with one broom apiece, taken on deck, and the Mate pointed forward to the forecastle head:

"Righto, lads! Start sweeping! When you get to the poop, let me know. I will have something else for you to carry on with."

Three or four weeks later, after having discharged the cargo in France, Bill and I were still sweeping those decks. Brooms - oh, how I hated the sight of them! That first day I was told to see the scuppers clear of coal. It took me hours to find out where they kept the scuppers.

After 5 p.m. tea, we were told to put the brooms away (until 7 a.m, the next morning) and to stand by for sailing at midnight. One by one the crew arrived on board. Firemen, sailors, cook and so on, and were they in a state. Dunston has always been able to offer refreshments to the sailor, be he coming or going. What sailor has not heard of the Cross Keys or The Keel? Later in the evening, Captain G.A. Whitfield, OBE, arrived on board, together with his wife and son, aged about seven, who were to make the voyage with us. Midnight saw the Sheaf Spear leaving Dunston outward bound, passing through the Swing Bridge. All the Robinson family was there to wave me goodbye and to wave back at them I had to put my head and arms through the poop railings. I was too small to see over the top rail.

Coal is known to be one of our greatest assets. To really get to know coal, leave Dunston outward bound at midnight, loaded to your marks with duff, while it's raining like nothing else on earth, battening down hatches and putting up topmasts, with a crowd of sailors very much the worse for wear and on your first voyage. Being December, ropes had to be stored away before reaching the open sea and when the ship passed through the piers at South Shields, it found yours truly on the forecastle head. How I ever found the apprentices' room that night or rather morning, I can't tell. Every time I put my foot down the deck appeared to come up to meet me. Upon reaching our accommodation, one look at Bill Hay told me what I must look like. Black! Filthy with coal dust and soaked through. A bath, yes, one half bucket of cold water and some Sunlight soap. Then to bed!

So much for the dreams of the apprentice who imagines himself in uniform, parading the bridge, telescope under his arm. Not in the tramp ship. True, we spent a lot of our time on the bridge but it was cleaning the brass work with the seat of our trousers hanging out!

"Rise and shine" on our first morning out we were called at 6.30 a.m. and after dressing, we swallowed what was supposed to be coffee. I should explain that the coffee pan was put on the galley at the beginning of the voyage and never removed until such time as it became too full of grounds that it was an impossibility to replenish it with water. This concoction just boiled and boiled day and night. Much the same happened to the tea pan. At the end of a couple of months, this was the real char and no mistake. You could almost get the spoon to stand upright!

At 7 a.m., we were told to turn to with the Bosun, a really fine sailor, T. O'Hara from North Shields. Our first job was coiling down mooring ropes under the forecastle head. We had not been at this job very long when, what with the ship pitching to a head sea, the smell of paint, ropes and all the odours one usually meets in the bow, I could feel my stomach starting to make tracks for Dunston and dry land again. What a rush on deck, I think Bill Hay made the rail first, but I was a damn good second. Of course, we would pick the wrong side of the ship and a chorus of voices, with no melody but with quite a few adjectives attached, informed us of our mistake. Our coffee and what appeared to be all the meals from the previous week were decorating the fore part of the bridge house. Try to picture two lads, fourteen years of age, faces as green as grass, lying over the rail, not caring if the ship floats, sinks or flies through the air, watching the water travelling aft and listening to the Mate's remarks about weak stomachs. I cannot say who had the weaker stomach, but I was throwing mine as far as Bill Hay at any rate.

At long last 8 a.m. arrived and we stopped work for one hour for breakfast. Billy Gee had just come off watch and collected our breakfast. Burgoo, with some black molasses in the centre. One look at this was enough. Then where was that lee rail we had heard about? Out of the room, not knowing whether to go right or left - too late! Now get a bucket and wash it up!
9 a.m. saw me turned in my bunk. 9.10 a.m. saw me turned out of my bunk. The mate had missed me.

Escorted by the Mate, whose opening remarks were always to the effect that we may have broken our mothers' hearts by coming to sea, but there was very little chance of our breaking his, we were taken on the foredeck carrying our brooms and told to continue sweeping operations.

Lying on the starboard side was the Board of Trade gangway. We swept around this very carefully and then ignored it, but not so Mr. Grisewood:

"Now then, you lads, stand that gangway on its side and sweep under it." Trying to lift the gangway proved too much for Bill and me, but Mr. Grisewood remarked that he was sure we could lift it if we really tried. "Bend down, grip the gangway and heave!" When you bend down like that the seat of your trousers draws rather tight. Ours did and Mr. Grisewood, with the end of a rope laid across our tight sterns, proved to us that we could lift that gangway.

Before 12 noon arrived, both Bill and I had overcome that feeling of seasickness and another feeling had taken its place - hunger! Noon brought the dinner bell, so off to the galley for the kits. Those were pretty tough ships and food was rather scarce compared to the standards of today. From one year's end to another we could tell exactly every day what would be found on the menu. Imagine a Sunday without plum duff or a Friday without salt fish. Two eggs a week, Tuesdays and Sundays. Today, tinned fruit and cream, cakes and on quite a number of ships, a bottle of beer with lunch (buy it yourself, of course!)

Our dining room was of course our living room. One of us had to sit on a bucket turned upside down, the settee being only large enough to seat two. He, the unfortunate one, did not spend any great length of time over his meals, those rims on a galvanized bucket are damned hard. After meals, we always took turns at being "Peggy" or the house maid and washed the dishes in the same bucket, then over the side went the dirty water and upon almost every occasion at least one knife or fork. We were often reduced to one spoon between three or four of us through this habit and it was only on the first day of sailing from port that we ever had a full set of cutlery. At times we were reduced to one pint pot each, as all our plates had also taken the voyage over the side. Every course came out of the same pot, soup, meat and duff, then after that a pot of tea or coffee. This of course washed out your pot for the next meal, about the only wash it had until maybe Saturday or Sunday, when we had to clean out the room.

As I have already remarked, the feeding was far from good and plenty, and one of our greatest treats was to help the steward take stores aboard. The steward, Mr. Caithness, had very poor eyesight, and apprentices, when allowed to approach within striking distance of the storerooms, take some watching. At one time the steward, Bill Hay and I were putting a hindquarter of beef in the icebox. Still attached to it was the ox tail, but before that beef was in the ice box, the oxtail was inside Bill Hay's shirt and that night we had ox tail for supper, around 1 a.m. when no one was around to smell it cooking.

During our first run to France, we, Bill Hay and myself, worked from 7 a.m. to 5 p.m. and then after a wash and tea we had to report to the officer on the bridge to learn how to steer. This usually lasted from 6 p.m. to 8 p.m., then we were free to go to our room and learn the compass by points or, as it was then known, how to box the compass.

For the time of year we had an exceptionally fine passage through the Bay of Biscay, then south down the coast of Portugal past those well-known islands "The Burlings". How often since have I altered course around those dangers to navigation. It was daylight when we passed through the Strait of Gibraltar, past that massive rock. Passing close inshore we watched, our eyes always turned to the port beam, the south coast of Spain, wondering what type of people lived amongst those dark brown hills or in those green fertile plains that ran down to the rocky shore washed by the blue - and it really is blue - Mediterranean. Then the rock itself, with the cement wall down the eastern side, stands for all the world like a lion in appearance, lying there guarding the entrance, steeped in both tradition and history. We could see the Royal Navy ships lying at the Mole; it made us very proud to be British.

Then came the day when the order was given to bring out our mooring ropes, and for Bill Hay and myself, it meant we were approaching our first foreign port - Marseilles, France. By this time we had got quite used to sweeping decks and little did we know that after discharge it all had to be done again.

I always remember how we were done down by one of the shore salesmen in that first port. They invade every ship, selling almost every commodity including postcards, not always bearing views of the city! One of these gentry sold me a bottle of lavender water, about a quart bottle for two shillings. Wonderful, what a bargain! With the bottle went strict orders not to open it until the present had been handed over in England. Believe me, they really know how to impregnate a cork with perfume and leave the coloured water without any odour whatsoever. Well, we live and learn. We were green in those days, but I am sure Bill would agree with me, we had more than our own back from "salesmen" before our four years were completed.

Marseilles was a really fine city to Bill and me, and the sweet shops and cake shops were something never to be forgotten. There were also other places of interest never to be forgotten by the sailors and firemen. Listening to the talk amongst the men I was surprised to learn that even in France these men knew a Mrs. Freeman and that there was also a public house "The Newcastle Arms". I have been back to Marseilles since and found they are both still there, still in business.

We left France two days before Christmas. We were bound for Cuba to load sugar for the USA. Then out came those damn brooms again. I had visions of not riding to the West Indies but of walking there, pushing that damned broom in front of me. Well, everything must come to an end. By Christmas Day, everything was cleaned, decks all washed and paintwork soogied after our coal cargo.

Christmas Day is one of the very few days that the sailor can claim as a holiday. That means no manual work to be done outside of sanitary duties, watches of course being maintained throughout. As a treat, the three apprentices were to have lunch in the saloon with the Captain, his wife and family, the mates and the radio officer or Sparks as they are known at sea. Rather a frightening event upon our first Christmas at sea, but we duly presented ourselves in our best (and only) uniforms to Mrs. Whitfield, who made it a very good day for us. On each of our plates was a large box of French nougat, so Santa Claus was still around. We had quite a dinner and were waited upon by the steward, who almost needed roller skates to cope with our outsized appetites. After all, we had to remember, that this meal had to last us until next Christmas Day. We were told by Captain Whitfield that we would be allowed to stay in the saloon listening to the gramophone in company with Mrs. Whitfield and their son, but first of all there was a small job for us. Off uniform coats, and into the pantry to wait upon the steward. Then wash all those dishes for the steward. Had we used all that crockery?

We spent a very pleasant afternoon in the saloon. Young Allan, the Skipper's son, became quite a charge of mine from that day. There was not a great deal of difference in our ages. I often acted as baby-sitter in the various ports that we visited, while his parents went ashore. His father and mother always remarked that the boy could really eat his supper when left with "Tich" as I was then known. Little did they realize that the greater portion of the supper ended up in the apprentices' room - or did they? Perhaps it was given as a short of inducement. At any rate, it was never wasted!

During the week between Christmas and the New Year of 1925 both Bill Hay and myself spent quite some time at the wheel learning how to steer. By this time we were past the Straits of Gibraltar and crossing the Atlantic to Cuba. With plenty of sea room, we were left alone at the wheel, and we needed plenty of room with the steering that we executed. Mr. Grisewood told me that he did not mind so much my trying to write my name with the wake of the ship, but to hell with my going back to dot the "I's"!

New Year's day I was asked if I liked to steer - "Oh Yes, Sir!" - "Well, go on watch at midnight." From that day until I finished my apprenticeship I was never again on day work at sea, always watches. For every apprentice on watch it means another AB on day work, more work done for the Mate and the upkeep of the ship.

1925

At sea in those times there were only the two deck officers: Mr. Grisewood, the 1st Mate, and Mr. N. Thompson, of Sunderland, the 2nd Mate. This meant that our watches were four hours on and four hours off, day and night. Watches at night comprised of wheel two hours, stand by one hour, and look out one hour or vice versa. As apprentices we had a job to keep awake at the wheel or on the lookout. At a later date one apprentice, who had the wheel from 4 a.m. to 6 a.m., actually fell so sound asleep he fell to the floor of the wheelhouse. The officer on watch, quite alarmed, thought the boy had collapsed and sent him off to bed right away. He went, believe me, was "doctored" later by the steward and spent two whole days in his bunk. All through falling asleep at the wheel! I know this to be a fact, for I was the apprentice!

When we arrived off Havana harbour we received our orders to proceed to our loading port of Cienfuegos on the southern coast of Cuba. Nothing outstanding had occurred on our voyage across the Atlantic to relieve the monotony of sea watches, but running around the Cuban coast, seeing flying fish and the dorsal fin of the shark for the first time, looking at those fine sandy beaches fringed with palm trees, what lad's imagination would not run riot? Shades of the pirates of the Spanish Main! At night, sailing along, under a full moon with the sea flat calm, and only the beat of the ship's engine to break the stillness, we imagined it to be a form of paradise with blue lagoons, tropical palms and bathing beauties, (perhaps this was due to the influence of the movies!) Even the offshore winds which carry the odours of decaying vegetation and other odours that are associated with tropical countries did not lessen our delight and enthusiasm.

To both Bill Hay and myself everything, being new and original, was attractive. We had both been told by Billy Gee and all the sailors that we would have to watch our hats when ashore as the practice was for the rather colourful and rather doubtful "ladies" to steal your hat then run home, hoping to heaven you would follow. With our minds on our hats and our eyes the size of dinner plates, we were off ashore as quickly as we could get all done up in uniform. Quite a place, plaza, bandstand, cafés, even open air movies, and people out walking in the cool of the evening with their children. Before I knew what was happening I was in the middle of a ring of little Cuban children while they danced around me playing "ring-a-ring of rosies". Owing to my being so small, they apparently thought I was one of the local children dressed up in naval uniform. And me a British seaman! Was my standard lowered! More so the next day when I was told the Captain and his wife had witnessed the whole scene.

Work while in port consisted mostly of stage-work over the side, on a plank, chipping and scraping the ship's side. First time over the side, I was far from happy at this job, remembering those dorsal fins we had seen. I could not swim a stroke - even to this day, and it's not for want of practice.

At the end of every day it was a great rush to get bathed, dressed and go off ashore. Before going ashore we apprentices had to ask the Chief Officer's permission.

Should we go and ask after getting dressed, we invariably got a job to do. When dressed we then had to report to the Mate, before going, fully dressed. Today this procedure has been dropped by quite a number of companies, I personally think much to the detriment of the Merchant Service. At least in those days we did wear the uniform, of which I for one am very proud, and we did wear it properly. We could always pick out the various shipping companies by their badge and buttons.

While loading in Cuba that first trip we were introduced to other not so pleasant forms of tropical life, namely the large sugar cockroach and mosquito. The sugar cockroach may be anything around three inches in length. Flying around the room he decides to do a three- point landing on your face or chest while you are trying to sleep at night. His back legs feel as if they have spurs on and believe me they are not very pleasant when they decide to make the round trip over your face!

If ever there was a pest, it is the mosquito, particularly that one individual that is left inside your mosquito net after you have doused the light and dived into your bunk. You can hear him flying around while you lie there in the dark, waiting for him to settle and strike - he will, without a doubt. Slap that place, then lie and listen again. The odds are that you missed him. If you get up and re-light the oil lamp more mosquitoes will be coming into your net, so what the hell, let him feed. On the other hand, you may, with luck, not have him in beside you, but during the night, your stern against the bunk board sticks out at the side of the net. This is it! One mosquito discovers this then shouts about it to all his ruddy pals. Boy, do they go to town. Then the next day you can hardly sit down for mosquito bites. One gets used to anything in time, they say. We certainly did with the various forms of life found on board the old *Sheaf Spear*.

Battening down again, over full hatches this time, not over coal but over brown sugar, we sailed, not in the cold miserable rain but under tropical skies, with the sun beating down on us, the sailors in much the same condition as when leaving the Tyne. As a crowd of sailors they were quite a good bunch, certainly I've sailed with much worse since. Before we finished loading, I recall, there was quite a commotion on the wharf. Two ABs, brothers from the port of Blyth, named George and Peter Gibney, had apparently been having that "one for the road", every road in Northumberland by the look of them! They were on the wharf trying to persuade a horse to walk up a rung ladder on to the deck. They said that they had bought it - possibly they had found it! Happily they were not successful and with a mighty whack on the stern of their new-found friend, they parted company.

Once the pilot was discharged, we were on our way once again, this time to Philadelphia, USA, around the western tip of Cuba and then up through the Straits of Florida. Assisted by the Gulf Stream running north we really made good time on this run, well off from the shore getting the full benefit from the current.

At this time Prohibition was still in full force in the USA and, as we moved up the coast of Florida, we passed quite a number of vessels, from old decrepit schooners to the latest of motor launches, all out on the rum-running racket. Even the old *Sheaf Spear*, as was later discovered, was carrying her share too, in the various sea bags and lockers of the crew. They had been there before.

The run from the West Indies to the northern ports of the USA can provide almost any type of weather at any time in the course of the voyage, from the flat calm and tropical skies to ice, snow and possibility of whole gales.

For quite some time after leaving Cuba, the work that we apprentices were assigned to was keeping the log clean of gulf weed. The ship was continually passing through this weed, supposedly coming from the Sargasso Sea, and it fouls the log every few minutes. One day you are working under tropical weather conditions then during the course of 24 hours the ship passes Cape Hatteras where you leave the Gulf Stream and meet the Labrador Current coming South. One day pants and singlet, the next overcoat and gloves. Summer and then winter within 24 hours of each other. You certainly require a good constitution to stand up to this.

By this time Bill and I were picking up quite a fair knowledge of seamanship and were beginning to get the idea we were hard cases. In fact we had picked up quite a number of sailor-like ways of expressing ourselves. We took good care that the Mate was not in the vicinity to hear us. Our Chief Engineer at the time was a Mr. Clargo, who upon hearing one of us use a profane word, always lectured to us on the subject, saying that there were quite sufficient words in the King's English to express your words and thoughts without resorting to the use of vulgar expressions. I have never forgotten either his lectures or the words he was talking about and I can never recall hearing Mr. Clargo using profane language, even whilst working under the most difficult conditions. Even though we had picked up this habit, we had not followed their example in other habits, we were still sticking to oranges, cakes and ice cream instead of anything stronger. Not that we did not change later, we did, but many years later.

At Delaware River mouth we embarked the American river pilot for the river passage to Philadelphia. In the outer reaches of the river Bill and I were allowed to take our trick at the wheel, but not when the river narrowed and navigation called for really good steering. When it came to my wheel I duly arrived on the bridge, the pilot took one look through the wheelhouse window, spotted me through the spokes of the steering wheel and asked me what I was doing there. "My wheel, Sir!" I replied. "Well, I'll be damned!" said the pilot, then "Left a bit, Sonny." To hear that pilot with his real American familiarity to the man at the wheel after the discipline of the officers was very strange to me.

Next stop on our way was the quarantine station where the doctor boards for the purpose of medically examining the entire crew of any foreign vessel arriving in the USA from any foreign port. The usual procedure is for the crew to pass through the saloon in single file, then remove your clothing and wait for the OK from the doctor. Once again my "manly stature" let me down. I was next in line to a rather large Geordie fireman, who was examined and passed. The doctor then turned to speak to the Captain, then turned to me. I was struggling to get my numerous coats, scarves, etc. off to show him what British seamen are built like (at the beginning) when he said, "OK, Son, don't bother, I'll take your word for it!"

Upon the vessel securing her full pratique or clean bill of health, we docked at the sugar refinery and, when all fast, the ship was searched by the customs for contraband such as liquor, etc. At this date, 25 years later, I cannot recall that they actually produced any after their search. I only remember that some of the searchers had certainly developed "fluid on the knees" or maybe the ship was rolling a lot when they came to pass down the gangway on their return to the quay.

Shortly after our arrival, our mail arrived on board. This, I must say, is definitely one of the greatest pleasures of a sailor's life, getting your letters from the people at home. What a treat, one nearly always reads the last one first, but who cares! They are all letters. Should you, the reader, have any friends at sea, you can rest assured a letter from you will be one of their greatest pleasures.

With our mail came our orders. We were now on time charter to Messrs. Moore and McCormick to run various cargoes from the USA to Cuba and sugar back to the USA for the next nine months. To us boys that did not mean a lot but to the men it was quite a different proposition. They had not anticipated such a long voyage.

Market Street in Philadelphia is quite some street of shops, movie houses and cafés. Almost anything from a needle to an anchor can be obtained there. One thing that we both missed was that cup of tea. We made up for this by spending almost our entire capital (about $2) on the wonderful ice cream and visits to the movies!

While we were discharging this sugar cargo I became very friendly with one of the engineers at the sugar refinery, who invited me to his home. There were quite a number of friends at his house too who were surprised at such a small boy with bright red cheeks being at sea. We visited Philadelphia a number of times on this time charter and it became quite the thing for me to spend my time at his house. I certainly enjoyed every visit.

When we completed our discharge we were ordered to Wilmington, Delaware, to load a cargo consisting mostly of steel parts, including locomotive wheels and axles. This then was to be our trade for at least nine months. General cargo from the USA to Cuba then sugar from Cuba to the USA, the round voyage taking four weeks.

Time passed rapidly for Bill and me on this run for there was always something new turning up. On the run south to Cuba, we were both on the same watch with Mr. Grisewood. One middle watch (12 to 4 a.m.) I was on standby when the Mate's whistle blew twice. This was the signal for me to run aft and read the log for the Mate. Upon hearing the whistle instead of going aft, I went up on the bridge and asked Mr. Grisewood for the loan of the electric torch to read the log. What a bellow! "Have we no oil lamps in the ship? Get aft and read that log!" I did so at full speed. When I returned and had told him what was on the log I was ordered to go forward, trim two hurricane lamps and bring them up on the bridge. Returning to the bridge with the two lamps trimmed and lit, the Mate then hailed the forecastle head where Bill was on the lookout, for him to come amidships. We were then presented with a hurricane lamp each, also the orders never to move without our lamps, day or night!

For weeks afterwards at sea, even during working hours in daylight wherever Bill and I went to work in the ship we had to carry our lamps with us. We never asked for his torch again!

With general cargo to discharge in Cuba, we usually had to visit practically every port in the Island, discharging parcels of cargo at each port. We would arrive in port at daylight, discharge all day then sail at sunset for the next port. During this running around Cuba, the three apprentices were the only deck department on watches with the two mates. We then had two hours wheel each, then four hours below, all the sailors being on day work for the purpose of driving the winches during discharge.

We did not get the opportunity of getting ashore very much in Cuba as we were frequently loading our cargo of sugar at anchor miles away from any town. There the only recreation was fishing, but we found this fascinating enough. Looking over the side we could see quite plainly the bottom of the ocean, see the sand rocks and weeds, with the fish and turtles moving through the water. When your line went over the side you could see the fish at any depth come up to your bait, and then make a dive at it. We caught some very queer fish out there!

Loading sugar alongside for any length of time, either Bill or I was always told off as watchman upon arrival. This meant night duty from 6 p.m. to 6 a.m. and what a job this was. Our hardest task was first to keep awake, next to keep a lookout for the "hombres" trying to stow away to the USA.

Poor Bill, no matter what he tried, he could never last out the whole night without falling asleep sometime during the 12 hours. Usually it was on the galley bench, but he really was not fussy; a box or the bag of potatoes outside the galley, he could even manage on that. He tried sleeping with the rolling pin under his neck so that he was bound to wake up through discomfort. But no, he slept in, forgot to call the Donkeyman for the purpose of raising steam then went around with a stiff neck for a couple of weeks. Ashore one trip in the States, he purchased a large Westclox alarm clock. Back in Cuba, the clock was taken into the galley and the alarm set for 5 a.m.. Then down to it. At 5 a.m. the steward got out of bed, no longer able to sleep for the ringing of the alarm, switched it off then woke Bill up. The alarm clock was at his head on the bench. Boy, could he sleep!

Stowaways, there were a very large number of these gentry, of almost every nationality too. They usually attempted to board the last night and they took some watching, for as hard as you were watching the beachcomber on the wharf, he was also watching you. Whilst you were doing this, his pals were climbing over the other side from a small boat. One individual attempted to board us in a very unusual way, up the ladder that was doing duty as a gangway. Bill was on his usual box outside the galley, half heard the footfalls on the wharf and being in the dark sat still, watching until the prospective stowaway was halfway up the ladder. Bill then quietly got up, took the box, which happened to be an empty plywood tea chest, balanced -his on both sides of the rung ladder and let go! The last Bill saw of that fellow he was trying to get the tea chest off his neck.

His head had gone right through the bottom of the empty box!

Taking stowaways into the USA was a very serious business for the captain of any ship, for stowaways discovered during the voyage were placed in detention ashore until the ship sailed, then put back on board again to be returned to Cuba, the costs of all meals and detention having to be paid for by the ship. Let this happen too frequently and even the best of masters would very soon have some sharp and to the point letters from the owners of the ship.

Whoever was watchman, Bill or I, we always called the other apprentice at 5 a.m., on job then till 7 a.m.. Oil all winches, remove the wedges from the tarpaulins, fill the sanitary tanks, make the coffee and call the men, all in one hour. You had to move around in those days. Overtime for apprentices was unknown, you were learning your trade, (the hard way.) One morning Bill called me at 5.30 a.m. I relieved him at 6 a.m. and he gave me the keys of the lazarette, saying, "Wait until the mates and men are around at 7 a.m., then tell the Mate I've locked some stowaways in the lazarette for him!" He was then into his bunk and fast asleep by 6.30 a.m.. At 7 a.m. I passed the information to Mr. Grisewood who sent for the police. When they arrived the lazarette was opened. Seven rather disappointed Russians were handed over. Bill had watched this crowd come on board at about 3 a.m. that morning and lower themselves into the lazarette. When the last one was in and the cover replaced Bill had walked up, put the bar over the top and locked them in. Nothing more to worry about that night!

When things were really serious regarding the number of stowaways attempting to board - and the nerve of some of them in doing so! - we were given an old revolver by Mr. Grisewood, unloaded, just to scare them with. This worked for quite a while until one morning Bill, rather worried, told me he had lost the gun - he had. He, as usual, had fallen asleep outside the galley, the revolver in his lap. The Mate who was unable to sleep, was out for fresh air and had removed the revolver without waking Bill. He woke him up the following day when he sent for him!

Every voyage to the USA, we had desertions or, as we called it, "skiving out". The better conditions and the wages for seamen in American ships were a great inducement to the British seamen. Long before we had completed that voyage, we had an entirely different crowd of sailors and firemen compared to that with which we had left England. Whenever we signed on men to take the place of the men who deserted, the ship had to provide everything for these seamen, bedding, blankets, plates, knives and forks. Even then the new men would take one look at the ship then beat it ashore again. So often did this happen, that the only way to prevent the ship being delayed was to order the men on board at the last moment, help them get their bags on board, then in with the gangway and sail. We practically had to shanghai the American seamen to get them to sail in a British tramp.

An attempt was made to improve the food by the purchase of a young pig alive, the idea being to feed it up, then slaughter it for fresh pork. For weeks, this pig lived in the centre-castle and fed on all the slops, in addition to the coal and old nuts and bolts that we gave it. The boys were always asking the steward when he was going to do the job of slaughtering. We were looking forward with gusto to pork chops. This pig was so lazy, we could walk over it before it would move at all, until the day came that its number was up. We were told off to assist the steward after 5 p.m. one night at sea to kill and dress the pig. Have animals any sense? That one had! When Bill and I went on the foredeck carrying some rope with which to truss it up, the pig was lying at the bottom of the ladder from the bridge deck. He took one look at us then up and off. We chased that animal around and around the foredeck until we managed to rope it like a cowboy would a steer. Then the steward made very short work of it with a knife. Result: we had pork! So much of it that we were grunting at each other. As the ship had no fridge, we had nothing else until it was all eaten. Since then I've never been able to look a pig in the eye without feeling very self-conscious!

Our time charter of nine months was drawing to a close. This trip we were loading what we thought was our last cargo of sugar for the USA. Then we had hopes of loading for the U.K. and home again. But it was not to be, we discharged the cargo then out into the river to an anchorage.

Mr. Grisewood called the three apprentices along to his room and asked would we like to earn some money - "Oh yes, Sir!" Our task then was to get out some black, white and blue paint, rig the staging round the runnel and paint it. We did so, received $10 each for the job, given permission to go ashore and were then told that the ship had been re-chartered for a further nine months on the same run by a firm in New York, the "Munson Line". Being chartered by this firm took the ship to the great port of New York every trip with our sugar cargo, then to load general cargo for the West Indies. This general cargo included everything - cars, food, powder, soap and upon one occasion, coal. It was some treat for the apprentices running to New York for we used to berth at the foot of South Street where the Mission to Seamen had their building. Many thanks, Mrs. Baster, for the really wonderful times you gave to those hard-up little ragamuffins. In the Mission, they had a room for apprentices only and quite a number of very nice and attractive young ladies would come down there every evening to make a party of it. Just sitting here thinking possibly those same young ladies will today be married and their daughters may be attending that room in the Mission, entertaining cadets and apprentices.

Never will Bill Hay and I forget South Street Mission and the ladies for, by this time, we were both getting ideas as to what Laddoes we'd grown up to be. On one occasion, Bill was making quite a lot of headway with one of the young ladies, sitting on a chesterfield with one arm along the back of the chesterfield, perfect gentleman (for this was the Mission), talking away to his partner. He commenced to play around with something at the head of the settee, then stuck his finger in it - it was a light plug for a reading lamp. I am willing to bet that never before or since has such language been heard in that Mission, just a blue flash and then Bill let her rip! We did live it down eventually!

Our one and only cargo of coal we loaded in Baltimore for Martinique, the French island in the West Indies, and, upon tying up there to palm trees at the head of the dock, we discovered that the distance between the ship and the quay was approximately 20 feet on both sides of the ship. Over this they placed gangways fore and aft then the stevedores came on board to discharge the cargo. Women, all rather dusky ladies, carrying baskets on their heads. That then was the method used to discharge the coal; they carried the coal in baskets down the gangways and dumped it on the quay.

During our stay in this port, the crew discovered how cheap they could get rum so there was very little work done by any of the crowd. They were off ashore. Mr. Grisewood had the life boats put into the water and gave us lads some real instruction in the handling of small sailing craft. For that instruction in those early days of my time at sea I shall always be grateful. Had I not had that instruction this story would never have been written, at least not by me!

Before our departure from the port of Martinique, we had a very unpleasant happening one night. Bill and I were standing on deck watching the crew of sailors and firemen returning to the ship, singing and rolling all over the road. They then started up the gangway and were halfway up, between the ship and the wharf, when a fireman lost his balance and went over the top into the dock. He hit the water, went down, and when he returned to the surface, yelled for help - he could not swim! Bill Hay went straight over the side into the dock. Forgotten were all those dorsal fins we had seen. After quite some time and difficulty, they were both landed on the wharf, the fireman carried to his bunk, attended to and sent off to hospital. Later we were informed that he had died there.

Upon his return to England Bill Hay was awarded the Lifesaving medal at the Newcastle Exchange.

When we arrived at New York Harbour on 20 December 1925, we were ordered to anchor off the Statue of Liberty awaiting at berth on the Brooklyn side. Of all the ports I have visited, New York holds the record for really cold winds and weather in the winter season. During the four days we lay there at anchor, we were employed working white paintwork. How we did not lose the use of our hands I don't know. At last the orders arrived for the ship to proceed alongside the discharging berth. Approaching the berth, it was discovered that all our deck steam lines were frozen - more trouble. After lighting fires from fore ward to aft, we eventually berthed and made fast, just right for Christmas. You never know your luck, Bill Hay and I were put on watch and watch for the entire time in port - keeping the pump for the domestic water from freezing up. Christmas Day arrived, dinner cooked for all hands, then it was discovered there was only one AB left on board, the remainder had "skived out". What a dinner that one AB had. A namesake of mine, "Spike" Robinson, was quite a card. During the week that followed, he managed to get himself arrested for disorderly conduct. He had apparently discovered a speak-easy, had maybe 6 or 7 over 8, then proceeded to Manhattan to one of the large offices there and decided to knock all the clerks there off their stools. His defence when arrested was that he never could stand shore people.

1926

On New Years Day 1926, we were once again loading general cargo for the West Indies. Before sailing, the last of our original deck crowd left the ship. The old bosun, Mr. O'Hara, was paid off, spent his last night living with us on board, then sailed for England the following day aboard one of the Cunarders. From then until we arrived home we had a crew of every nationality under the sun.

Throughout the eighteen months spent on the Eastern seaboard of the USA, we on the *Sheaf Spear* were very fortunate with the weather. Not that we had fine weather throughout, for on two occasions we had to ride out a hurricane. That is the tropics for you. In the forenoon, you can have really wonderful weather, sun shining and a gentle breeze, then afternoon you notice that all the breeze has dropped, the sea oily with a heavy swell commencing, then out come the hurricane warnings over the radio and by midnight the ship is head into the wind and sea, doing everything but turn over. If you are lucky, the next day conditions are normal once again; we must have been lucky. The fact that we had an exceptionally good seaman as Master, as Captain G. A. Whitfield possibly saved us from the worst of the weather during those trying times.

This engaging of a new crew every visit to the USA certainly introduced us to every form of humanity. Good, bad and indifferent, men with no hopes or ambitions, men on the run, men with no country or even home to call their own, clean seamen and the other kind. With the exception of the steward, we had also a new catering staff, new cook and new boy. They occupied the room next to ours and, if ever a boy was bodily dirty, this specimen was. I am sure he went without even a wash for weeks, his clothes just about stood up alone with grease and he had never seen a hairdresser since being a child. One evening Bill and I decided to do something about it. The galley boy, as was his usual practice upon finishing in the galley at 6 p.m., just flopped out in his bunk together with a wild-west magazine. We let him have about half an hour to get properly settled, then we paid him a visit!

While Bill held him down I went to work on his hair with a pair of scissors. Had he not struggled so much, he might have had quite a decent haircut, but he just would not keep still, therefore the hair I could get at just had to come off. After his haircut we then cut his trousers up - he still had them on when we started but not when we finished. To end the party, Bill and I let him have the full contents of a bucket of dirty soapy water, then we beat it!

About one hour later we were sent for to report to Captain Whitfield. On arriving there we found the galley boy together with his haircut and what was left of his trousers, putting his case before the Captain, who lectured Bill Hay and I, ordered us to supply a new pair of trousers to replace those we had destroyed. Then the Captain thanked us for a very well-spent half an hour; he had enjoyed it too!

We continued on this trade for the "Munson Line" until August 1926 and then in Baltimore, Maryland, we received the wonderful order "Load coal and proceed to

London". The general strike at home was then causing ships to "carry coals to Newcastle".

Never was a ship battened down quicker than the *Sheaf Spear* that trip. Most of the work was done by the two mates and three apprentices; the only ones left out of the original deck crowd, then we sailed for home.
Anyone who has spent any length of time away from the land of their birth will be aware what it is like to return. What a thrill it was for us to be passing first the Wolf Rock then the Lizard Head, then to steam up the English Channel. Even the old ship was going faster than ever before. You look at those chalk Cliffs of Dover and you almost feel you own them. They are part of you, you think within a matter of hours you will once again be handling and spending pounds, shillings and pence instead of dollars, quarters, nickels and dimes. And, shortly, with luck, we may be on our way home for a few days leave.

At Gravesend, at anchor awaiting a discharging berth, we were visited by the marine superintendent, Captain Clarke. "Tubby" as he was known to us, was also feared by us boys. If he started off around the fore deck we beat a hasty retreat aft. In himself, a fine seaman and a gentleman. At the outbreak of the 1914 war Captain Clarke, who was then in Hamburg, as Master of one of Messrs. Souters ships, I believe the old *Sheaf Field*, refused a pilot. It looked very like internment, but not for Captain Clarke. Let go and off! They never caught him yet, he is still a very active man. I had the pleasure of renewing our acquaintance recently in the port of Falmouth. I had to put in there whilst I was master of the present *Sheaf Field* through heavy weather and who should jump on board but Captain "Tubby" Clarke. Almost 25 years had elapsed since we last met. What a pleasure to sit in my room and talk of old times.

Discharging berth in the London River was the Erith Coal Wharf and, after having tied up, there was a general exodus from the ship, everyone anxious to be off home. Amongst the apprentices, only two out of the three were to be allowed any leave, so Bill Hay and I tossed for it. I lost. Billy Gee, being senior, had about two months to do to complete his apprenticeship, so he was also entitled to leave. They were to go off the following morning. That afternoon Bill and I had a walk ashore and upon our return spotted a boy with a school boy cap on his head jumping on and off the gangway. We of course told him to clear off. He was the new apprentice, H. L. Banks. Good heavens, thought Bill and I, they are sending children to sea these days, real hard cases, Bill and I.

Should you ever become a seaman and wish for a spell at home, don't take coal to London. Discharging there is only a matter of hours. They can certainly handle coal, and our stay was only a few hours alongside. Then the vessel needed to dry-dock and repair. Owing to the general strike, we were ordered to Rotterdam. Before sailing, the third engineer, who had been on the ship for quite a while, was promoted to second engineer and then started to celebrate his promotion. Upon being ready to sail, "Stand by" was rung on the telegraph with Captain Clarke standing on the wharf to see us off. The second engineer took one look at the telegraph, said "Hie! That's full ahead!" We were still made fast to Erith jetty!

The new second engineer, although a stranger to us, was a much younger man. Then we crossed to Rotterdam to Walton's Dry dock for about two weeks dry docking. During our stay in Rotterdam, the missions to seamen were very popular with all the apprentices. They supplied free teas, and the apprentices from almost every ship met there. One afternoon Bill Hay and I were talking to other apprentices when we were asked by one lad how many trips we had done. "Just the one!" was the reply. We were then told that we would soon settle down after two or three trips. The fellow who was telling us, had exactly eight months sea time in. We had almost two years.

Before we completed repairs, Captain Whitfield left the ship for a holiday, Mr. Grisewood being promoted master and a Mr. S. Dring joining us as Chief Officer. Our next voyage was to be a run to the USA. for coal then back to the U.K. -just a short trip.

We sailed for Rotterdam - same ship but an entirely different crew, the three apprentices being the only members who had been on the previous voyage.

The voyage to Baltimore was remarkable for its fine weather although we took some time to make the voyage. Upon arrival, Captain Grisewood was relieved of his command. He returned in the ship as a DBS, Mr. Dring taking over the command.

The deck crew were all signed on in Well Street, London. Among the ABs was one elderly man by the name of Peters. The bosun who runs the seamen, could never hit it off with Peters. They were always at loggerheads with each other throughout the passage out. If there was a dirty job you could bet that Peters would get it.

Upon arrival in the USA and Captain Dring taking over command, the necessity of getting a new 1st Mate arose. The 2nd Mate possessed only a second mate's ticket and could not take the first mate's berth. Captain Dring went aft into the sailors' forecastle and asked if any of the men possessed a certificate. Peters spoke up, "Yes, I hold a master's - square rigged!" He was asked if he would take the first mate's berth until the ship arrived in the U.K. - he did.

Moving all his gear amidships, he asked me if I had a pocket whistle. I had not, but obtained one from the 2nd Mate. He immediately blew his whistle, the watchman came to his room and his first order was "Send that so-called bosun along here, at once!" Were we going to have a trip home now!

Loading completed, pilot on board and off once again, bound for the U.K. I myself had hopes of getting home for a few days leave this time. In company with the *Sheaf Spear*, there were three other British merchant ships, all loaded with gas coal for the U.K.; the weather being then fine and clear all the way to the outer pilot station. There we discharged the pilot and "Full away" for England.

Within the next 24 hours, we had a great change in the weather conditions; overcast sky, strong to gale force wind and rough confused sea. We received radio messages that a hurricane had struck the American coast and had re-curved out into the Atlantic. We knew it for we were on the receiving end.

Hove to for days, some of the crew sleeping in the engine room, others that were aft were unable to get amidships owing to the seas that were smashing aboard every few minutes. Our galley was completely washed out and our two lifeboats, they were only shells now, forward. There was not a wire reel left on the forecastle head, they had been washed overboard. To stand on the bridge or at the wheel and watch the bow fall into the trough with a massive sea ahead made anyone wonder if he would ever come up again. SOS signals were received, but under the circumstances there was absolutely nothing we could do to assist. There must have frequently been times when Captain Dring was thinking we may be the next one to send out for help. He was having a very hard trip, this his first time in command.

When we did get the chance to sleep we just lay down where we were, wet clothes did not matter, that was a mere detail.

In time, a lull in the conditions was felt and the first job was to get the galley fires going for the purpose of a hot meal. Everything was going fine in that direction until about half an hour before the meal was ready. We shipped a sea over the starboard side of the bridge deck. This sea carried all the mid-ship sails away, also the galley door and out the port galley door came the cook, pans and dinner. Eventually conditions improved, the wind decreased as did the sea, and we were then able to take stock of the damage done by the gale.

With a cargo of gas coal, ventilation was a necessity. Our ventilators had not been able to withstand the terrific pounding from the heavy seas and there was a good quantity of water in the holds. We made a course for the nearest harbour, that of Queenstown, and it was with a great sigh of relief from all on board when our anchor went down in Queenstown Bay.

Orders received upon arrival were that the ship had to proceed up river and discharge the cargo in the port of Cork. Upon the quay waiting for the ship's arrival were Captain Clarke and Captain Whitfield. No sooner were they on board than I was up on the lower bridge asking Captain Clarke if I could go off for a spell of leave at home. He immediately shouted that I had already been home from London. I told him very meekly that I had lost the toss that time and that I had not been home for nearly two years. "Very well, sonny, away you go!" "What about some money, sir? His reply to this I remember very well. It would not appear well in print.

Some journey, from Cork to Newcastle. By the time I arrived in the Central Station, Newcastle, half my period of leave was over. Then five rather hectic and wonderful days at home, spinning quite a few tall stories and putting my foot in it at times when a sailor-like expression slipped out. Once again that train journey back to Cork to re-join the ship in the Rushbrook dry dock.

Billy Gee, the senior apprentice, had by this time completed his four years on board. More than four years in just over two trips with something like two days at home during the four years. He said then that he intended to stay right there, stand on the quay to wave goodbye, then turn his back on the sea and every ship that sailed there and never would he return to sea - he never did!

To fill the berth of Billy Gee, we received one more apprentice making four in all: Robinson, Hay, Banks and Wright. One more up-turned bucket at mealtimes! We had a portable table made for us, very portable, every time anyone passed by that table it collapsed. That table very soon went overboard, after having had to clean the floor up on two or three occasions.

During the first years of our apprenticeship Captain Whitfield had a parrot on board. It later died, from starvation, I think. It was a habit of Captain Whitfield's to keep this parrot and cage out on the lower bridge and, at 11 a.m. every day, half an apple was jammed between the wires of the cage. At 11.05 either Bill Hay or I had that half apple. That parrot was very unlucky where fresh fruit was concerned.

The following year was spent tramping throughout the seven seas, every port and country on the map: Montreal, Durban, Basra, Persia, Spain, USA and a whole lot more thrown in for good measure. At last came the good news: we were to go to the Tyne for dry-docking and repairs, the possibility of at least a month at home. Were we thrilled at this news for we had had a rotten thin time with the food situation, a new steward had kept us right down to our bare rations until we were really out for blood. Once the ship's head was on the course for home we settled the matter of a little extra food very effectively.

One night at about 7 p.m., we were all in the room, three of us remained there while the other lad went for the steward with the story that Bill Hay felt sick, would he come and have a look at him? He did! We let him in there, locked the door and explained to the steward, who was only a little chap, that he, the steward, was the one who was going to be terribly sick if we did not get more food. We really convinced that fellow and our food improved from that day.

England again! The Tyne of all the ports too, nothing could be finer. We were docked in the Newcastle dry dock at Hebburn for one month, all hands paid off and the apprentices to share the month, half on board and half on leave. Bill Hay and I took the first two weeks on board, Banks and Wright the last two.

When Captain Clarke arrived on board, we asked what we were going to do about food, no cook or steward being on board. Wonders never cease, we were given the keys of the storeroom! At the end of the first week, the company checked the storeroom with the surplus store list sent in on arrival. After that we had to give up the key of the stores and arrangements were made for us to get our meals ashore. We went once for a meal to arrange a little matter of money, after that we always brought our meals on board with us and collected the amount paid for our meals from the lady who was told off to supply them. She was a good sport and we were always hard up for cash!

Buying our dinner one day in one of the local shops, the person serving us asked if we were on a collier, paying our grub for the week. Oh no, this was just our dinner - how I wish I had that appetite today.

Time flies and our month at home passed very quickly. Then off again; this time to the continent, then out to Delagoa Bay and Durban. At Antwerp we loaded a very mixed cargo comprising sand, steel pipes and sardines. We, the lads, very soon had a case of sardines in the room, then the supper was sardines on toast for weeks afterwards. Whilst discharging in Delagoa Bay, we had more fruit than we could possibly manage - a bunch of bananas for an old shirt. Those natives can wear anything. Bill Hay said that shirt was old, believe me, it was old and had long since ceased to be recognizable as a shirt! They took it.

Durban has always been a very popular port of mine. In those days Bill and I really got on the job of working things out to time between the two missions. One mission, the "Flying Angel", would have a film show and no supper, the "Sailors' Society" would have a musical evening and supper. We found that if we attended the film show, then ran through gardens, back streets and alleyways, we could make the supper just as the musical evening was drawing to a close. Did we have to travel at speed, often so much out of breath we could hardly say thank you for the bun! Those two missions are still going strong. Good luck to them for there have been lots of families in this country of ours that have enjoyed the food parcels they sent off. The sailor just pays the amount, the mission people do the rest and we were always sure that the parcels we paid for would get home. A lot of our time in Durban was spent fishing for eels; massive conger eels. We caught quite a number and then were puzzled what to do with them, but we soon found a use for them! One of the engineers returned on board, under the influence and was put to bed, out for the count. Here was a use for the eels which were still struggling to get back into the harbour. We put them into bed with the engineer, who apparently fought them all night. He was later landed in hospital, sick and a very bad nervous case. I do hope that, should he read this book, he will forgive both Bill Hay and myself for what to us that night was just a silly trick.

Coal once again; we loaded a full cargo at the Bluff, in Durban, next to the whaling station. This cargo was for Perim Island; we were off for the Red Sea, where Scotsmen go to fill their fountain pens. There is one part of the world there that is definitely red, it's red hot, and what a wonderful place Perim was in those days. I have never returned! In those days it was purely sand and more sand, with a camel or two lying around. We lay there for about 10 days discharging, spending most of our time in the swimming pool. Here I really did swim; owing to the excessive salt one has quite a job to sink. That just suited me, for I have always been good at that "sinking".

Between Perim Island and our next port of Basra, in the Persian Gulf, our job was that of cleaning holds, and after coal cargo, we were to load liquorice root for the USA. To do this work, all the clothing we wore was one pair of shorts, out with the hose and the heat of the day very soon dried out the holds. This voyage through the Red Sea would quite possibly be very interesting and enjoyable to the passengers of a liner, sitting under the awnings, sipping a very nice iced drink and telling the girlfriend all about the natives and their habits, not mentioning your own, of course. But what about that other fellow, that fireman who spends eight hours a day in front of three forced draft boilers and their furnaces. I know that up on deck the temperature is usually 100 degrees plus in the shade and there is no ruddy shade. What must it be like down there! It was known as "blood money". I have seen Arabs give it up and Geordie sailors take their place. Strange, is it not?

Our stay in Basra was of very short duration for which we were truly thankful. The hours of work there, owing to the excessive heat, being from 3 a.m. to 8 a.m. Only then you spend the remainder of the day under an awning, trying to find a breeze. Our cargo of liquorice root was for the Tobacco Co. of Baltimore - quite a trip, Basra to Baltimore.

Once again through the Red Sea to Suez, then the passage through the Suez Canal, sand and sun and lots of both. Here one can see the ancient and modern side by side, for upon the road running alongside the Canal one sees the Arab on the camel, robes flying out behind, or the ass loaded to capacity with the owner perched on top, being overtaken by the motor car or armoured truck with some Tommies on patrol. At one end Suez, at the other Port Said where we were invaded by merchants of every type, all trying to sell you something and the things they have to sell! Some trying to tell you your fortune or cut your hair, but they all have the same idea and that is to do you, and do you properly!

Taking on board coal bunkers in Port Said for the voyage to Baltimore, the ship was invaded by an army of natives who, with built-up stages from the coal barge to the deck of the ship, proceeded to pass baskets of coal by hand. This method, whilst very primitive compared to the present day method of shutes and cranes, was actually a very quick form of bunkering and it was not very long before we were clear of Port Said and on our way to Baltimore.

Both Bill and myself were putting in quite a lot of studying, for we were now getting towards the end of our apprenticeship. During this time I was taking the 4 p.m. to 8 p.m. watch on the bridge and, with Captain Whitfield always in the offing, I picked up a fair amount of navigation and seamanship, both theoretical and practical. This I am sure stood me in good stead later when I sat for BOT certificates. Remembering this, I have always had the senior cadet or apprentice on the bridge upon every possible occasion, allowing the boy to use his own judgement when called upon to alter course, check the compass error or in the taking of sights. I do sincerely hope that they benefited by the practice when they came up before the examiners of masters and mates.

Baltimore to us was better known than quite a number of our ports in England for we had certainly been there on a number of occasions. We had a number of shore friends with whom we spend many a pleasant evening, visiting movies, parties and going into the country for runs in the automobile. Bill and I were beginning to think American, we had by this time become quite accustomed to being called "honeys" and we always enjoyed our visits to the USA. Over there, they said, "Work hard. Live hard. And play hard." I think it's a fine idea too.

The ship, after discharging her cargo of liquorice root, was ordered to Mobile, Alabama for a cargo of dressed timber for West Africa. This would be the last trip for both Bill Hay and myself. West Africa, then home!

Our cargo here was not only stowed under hatches, but also on deck both forward and aft. The mates and apprentices were all engaged in building channels for our rod and chain steering gear along the after deck. Thank heaven that we made a good job of this for after a few days at sea bound to the African coast, we ran into the tail end of hurricane. Everything happens at night! It was all hands on deck, first to put the relining tackle on the rudder head, tighten up the kicking strop and screw down the brake on the old Taylor Pallister Quadrant! One could ask quite a number today to reeve off a relieving tackle without finding anyone capable of doing so. No sooner was this task completed than out again. The steering gear had carried away, one link had parted. This meant crawling through the channels we had built putting in a spare link. This was done by the bosun; all hands waiting at the end of the deck cargo for him to come out of the channel again. A very unpleasant job for anyone, crawling through a channel on hands and knees to find the broken link, with all the deck cargo above you creaking and groaning, moving slightly to every roll of the ship, wondering if it is going to hold until you get out. We spliced the main brace good and properly when that job was finished and the ship once more on her course for Dakar.

Before we arrived at our destination, the ship had developed quite a list and, upon arrival, we were ordered to unload our deck cargo into the harbour before going alongside. Once alongside, out came the stages and the usual job of painting over the ship's side. In this port, we had the starboard anchor hanging outside the hawse pipe, almost down to the water. The ordinary seaman was given the job to paint the cable and anchor and, given a pot of black paint and brush, he went on with the job. At 12 noon we were surprised to see him walking along the quay with the water dripping from his clothes. We asked if he had fallen into the docks. "Oh,no!" He had commenced painting from the top of the cable downwards instead of from the anchor upwards. At 12 noon he was on the anchor, with all wet paint above him, he dived into the dock and swam to the side steps.

Once again we were in the tropics with all that one finds there: heat, smells, disease, mosquitoes and fever. Our regular dope was quinine, and lots of that. A good number of the crew were down with malaria, Bill Hay being one of them. It was a regular sight to see the old man with the thermometer in his hand doing the morning rounds or at night, dressing malaria boils on our legs and arms with hot lint. It is difficult to express my thanks and gratitude for all that Captain Whitfield did for Bill Hay and myself; not only in the way of instruction in seamanship, but also for his care and attention to the welfare of the apprentices who served under his command. He taught us to live as men, to respect our uniform and calling. He also taught us to obey. One can never command unless he has first learnt to obey.

Upon completion of discharge, we proceeded from Dakar to Bordeaux for a general cargo. This was also for the West African coast starting at Dakar. We discharged small parcels of cargo at various ports down the coast to Lagos, arriving at that port in December 1928.

This was the great day for Bill Hay and me, 3 December 1928. We were sent for by Captain Whitfield. When we entered his room, he produced a bottle and three glasses, addressed us as Mr. Hay and Mr. Robinson. We were now finished our apprenticeship and from that day would be paid the rate of an AB, £9 per month. We then had our first drink of liquor with Captain Whitfield. He wished us the very best of health, success in our exams and for the future, then told us we could have the remainder of the day free. We celebrated in no mean style and it was only after a lot of persuading that I managed to prevent Bill from buying a racehorse that night. What he was going to use for money, I don't know.

Loading the ore, we lay at anchor riding to a heavy ground spell with the ore barges scraping and bumping alongside. All the cargo was put on board by the ship's watches, with natives filling and emptying the tubs of ore.

From Segundi to Axim, where we landed the natives who had worked the cargo. Then we were off for home with one call to make: at Dakar to replenish the bunkers. Homeward bound is the best part of any voyage to anyone, and to us on that trip nothing could have been better. Every mile was one less to do, the navigation books were never off the table, we went around the decks repeating the rule of the road, or articles. We were going to the BOT full of knowledge, or so we thought, until we got there!

Never shall I forget that arrival home in the Tyne, paying off at South Shields with one month 28 days AB's wages, then off to the office of Messrs. W.A. Souter & Co for our £5 bonus. When we presented ourselves at the office, Mr. A. Lane asked what we were there for and without any hesitation we told him £5! We were presented with £5 each, given our indentures signed by Mr. W.A. Souter to the effect that we had served four fifths of our time at sea. Then Mr. Lane wished us success in our examination and instructed both of us to report to him when we had obtained our second mate's certificate.

1929: School and AB

Our next move was to enrol at the Marine School, South Shields, as students for the second mate's examination. Every day I travelled from Gateshead with my little attaché case to attend school, or rather that was my intention when I left Gateshead. But spending the day in South Shields in the company of Bill Hay, it was very little schooling that was done.

At that time the girls in Woods clothing shop opposite could semaphore a damn sight better than those of us in school going through our signals. Mornings were usually spent sitting in the Rona café, drinking coffee until lunchtime, with about one hour in school. Then the lunch hour or hours we paraded King Street and Ocean Road, I think for the purpose of allowing the other sex the opportunity of seeing what a wonderful Merchant Navy England possessed. Wonderful in our eyes, what the girls thought may have been entirely different. Nearly everyone of them had brothers in the service and the majority of the residents of South Shields know ships and seamen.

Everything was just right to us. No early rising, no watches or mate to chase you around, possibly it would have been a lot better for us had we had someone to chase us, for after two months had passed at this rate of living, our knowledge of navigation, etc., had not increased to any great amount, but our financial status had decreased remarkably. We still paraded around South Shields, but I for one was getting nearer Mill Dames and the Shipping office every day, then it came. I was broke! To find a job, having no certificate, there was only the forecastle and an AB's job for it, so off to the Shipping office and a tramp around the various docks looking for a job and being interviewed by chief officers. I eventually obtained a promise of Quartermaster on the SS *Port Caroline*, and ordered to be at South Shields 10 a.m. the following morning for signing on.

Upon arrival at the shipping office, I was pulled up by the Seamen's Union delegate who asked for my union book. All I had was my indentures - no union book! Off to Unity Hall where I was asked to join the Union before getting this job. Every seaman had to obtain a PC 5 before passing the doctor. This PC 5 was obtained from the Union and presented to the Shipping Federation. To join the Union, I had to have £3. This amount was out of the question. All I had that day was £1-10s-0d, a pound note and a ten shillings note. The Union official asked me how much I could afford, until I had obtained an advance note. Having two notes loose in my pocket I of course said 10/-. What a job, trying to feel the difference between a 10/- note and a £1 note. Well, trust to luck, I pulled out a note and my luck held - it was the 10/- note! Everything was then arranged - Union book and PC 5 and I was signed on the SS Port Caroline as quartermaster.

I joined this ship at Wallsend Slipway and we left for speed trials the following day. This was an entirely different ship to the *Sheaf Spear*, and I very soon found this out, for, when it came to my wheel, I relieved the quartermaster and the order was given "Hard-a-port". I pulled the wheel over, thinking at the same time that it was very stiff and heavy. I held the wheel over until the order was given to "Ease the helm", then I let go. The wheel of course spun back to amidships rapping my fingers as it did so. The officer on the bridge asked if I had ever been with Telemotor Steering before. I had not, but very soon settled down to this new type of steering gear.

After our speed trials, we returned to the Tyne for a further 48 hours, then sailed for Middlesbrough. The ship was taking on board cargo for Australia at various points in England and the Continent. We visited Middlesbrough, Antwerp, Hull, Hamburg and London. During our time in port, we, the quartermasters, had to maintain a gangway watch, 6 hours on then 12 hours off. On gangway duty, we had to wear the uniform of the C&D Line, a blue jersey with the letters C&D across the chest and the little round blue naval hat.

In all ways this ship was different from the *Sheaf Spear:* size, speed and crew. There appeared to be so large a crew that after three weeks on gangway duty I was still stopping strangers from coming on board, to find out that they were firemen, sailors or stewards and all crew members.

Arriving at King George docks, London, in the early hours of the morning, we received a shock. We were all told to pack our bags and were paid off, given our railway warrants back to South Shields and dispensed with, for we had only been engaged for the coastal run. The deep-sea crew members took over then.

On pay for three weeks, what money I had to draw was very little. We had visited both Antwerp and Hamburg and it is always expensive for me when I visit these ports: there are so many attractive and delightful ways of spending your wages. Returning home, I had to find another berth in the very near future, so back again to South Shields.

Shipping was beginning to slacken off. Freights were falling and to get an AB's berth was not an easy matter. It was then the custom to present your discharge book to the mate, who, if satisfied with your book and abilities, promised you a job upon the vessel opening articles. There were numerous incidents of the real humour of seamen in the face of unemployment. Incidents such as that of men handing their books to the mate with the remark "Here you are, sir. Read this one, it's one of the Edgar Wallaces!" Or the story of the men who, after being taken on, and much to the disgust of the Captain and Mate, worked at the two speeds Dead Slow and Stop. Then, about a week before the ship arrived in the U.K., they had worked like slaves. Upon arrival, they had presented themselves at the Mate's door, very well behaved and only too anxious to do anything he might ask, they asked could they have their jobs the following voyage. The Mate, with the antics of this crowd when in Rosario still very fresh in his memory, told them in a few very well chosen phrases just what their chances were of every getting another job from him!

Shortly afterwards I was fortunate enough to be standing outside of the Shipping Office, when a call was made for an AB for the SS *Medjerda*. Only one AB was required, I offered myself for the berth and was accepted, signed our Articles and was told off to join immediately. About three hours later, I was on board, found my bunk and the remainder of the deck crowd. I asked why the AB had left the ship, when work was so scarce. I was told he had jumped over the side at night on the voyage home! "Dead men's shoes!"

The run or voyage for these ships was from the northeast coast of England to Savonna in Italy, Savonna to North Africa for iron ore to the Continent to discharge, then back to the northeast coast for more coal.

My first trip was in the Second Mate's watch, Mr. Joe Storey of South Shields, and we very soon found out we were both acquainted with the same people, giving us a source of conversation during watches. These watches, spent on an open bridge, no wheelhouse or shelter, could be very cold and bleak and, at the end of a two hour turn at the wheel in wintertime, one usually made a rush for the galley to stand in front of the fire and thaw out, passing remarks about "Brass Monkeys" at the same time.

The ships on this run were very heavy regarding hatches and beams. Nearly all the ports we visited had a twenty-four hour working day. This meant off hatches and beams, then stand by to replace the same; there was very little free time in port for any of the deck hands. This did not cause any of the men to throw the job up and go ashore on the hopes of getting an easier and lighter ship, for we all knew only too well that a depression was just starting in the merchant shipping of England and jobs were very few and far between.

At a later date the Second Mate was transferred to the SS *Tunisia* and, when I heard from him that an AB was also required, I changed ships too; both vessels being of the same company and in the same trade.

During my time on the SS *Tunisia* one voyage I shall always remember was during the winter of 1929-30. The ship was returning homewards with an iron ore cargo, passing through the Bay, with a moderate NW gale blowing, my wheel was midnight to 2 am. Standing there I could hear the seas coming on board over the weather bulwarks, she was shipping some heavy water at times. Suddenly we took one sea over the starboard side with quite a thump on the No 2 hatch. Mr. Storey looked over the fore part of the bridge and there were No 2 derricks swinging from port to starboard and back again every time we rolled. They had been carried away by the sea and dropped on top of No. 2 hatch; ripping tarpaulins, smashing hatches and leaving the hold open to any sea that came on board. It was immediately the order "All hands on deck!" and it certainly meant all hands, from the Captain to the Boys.

We had to strip the torn tarpaulins from the seven hatches, make fast two heavy derricks; all this to be done in the dark with water coming over every few minutes.

The ship was hove to. In taking off the tarpaulins, I was shining an electric torchlight in the hatch wedge while another seaman used the hammer to knock them out. He was certainly a poor shot with a hammer and I told him so. It turned out to be Captain Hatch, the master of the ship. We then changed over, he shining the light and myself using the hammer. With everyone working like slaves, no time was lost nor can any ship's company afford to lose much time with the main hatch stove in during a winter gale in the Bay of Biscay or anywhere else for that matter.

Everything comes to an end and we managed to get everything squared up and secured, the ship put back on her course again, then hot rum for all hands. With that and a pint pot full of tea, we very soon forgot the uncomfortable position we had all been in for a few hours and I am sure that within 24 hours the majority of the crew had forgotten all about this incident. It was just one of those things that could happen - and does - to anyone.

After completing three voyages in this vessel I had pulled together enough money to have one quick shot at my second mate's examination with no fooling around. Together with being ashore out of work, no wages, and my mother to look after too, it would have to be a very quick turn around.

This time instead of going back to the South Shields school where I knew lots of seamen, I enrolled at the Newcastle school of Mr. William Nellest. Knowing hardly anyone there I very soon got down to some really hard studying. I had always studied at sea and this certainly stood me in good stead for in a very short time I put in my papers at the BOT offices and presented myself for examination.

First, another sight test; then the following week was spent at the Board of Trade writing up papers on navigation, chart-work, methodology and quite a number of other subjects. Then came the signals consisting of Semaphore, Morse, Flag Waving (since disbanded) and

Morse signalling with the signal lamp. The toughest part of the examination is without doubt the seamanship room, otherwise known as orals. I was before the senior examiner, Captain Robson, and after a very uncomfortable hour, I was informed that I had been successful in passing my Second Mate's examination. Did I feel good, at last, a certificated officer! And where were those ships that required a Third Mate!!!??

It took me more than four years to obtain a berth as Third Mate.

With a brand new certificate, No. 26887, in my pocket, my head in the clouds and my chest sticking out, I commenced going from one office to another during the daylight, writing letters to various Shipping companies at night, looking for that officer's berth. Then I discovered that there were hundreds of certificates of all ranks, doing just what I was doing - looking for work, any work.

Once again, that same old complaint, short of money, was right with me. There was only one alternative, get an AB's berth for a while until conditions in shipping improved. Many seamen holding certificates spent quite a while as ABs during this depression.

At South Shields shipping office I obtained an AB's berth on the SS *King Egbert*, bound for Australia. My wages were £8-2s-0d a month. I was told by Captain Poulgrain, the master of the ship, to take my certificate with me on the trip as anything may turn up while abroad.

The *King Egbert* was my first motor ship and I found it quite a treat to get away from coal and coal dust for a while. Also the fact that we were bound for Australia was a great attraction, never having been "down under" before.

During the run in ballast to Port Pirie in the Spencer Gulf, our time was spent down the holds removing sealing and scraping and painting the tank top - an ideal trip from the First Mate's point of view, but to the deck crowd, day after day spent with a scraper or a red lead brush in one's hand it gets very monotonous. Every night, I used to get out that certificate just to make sure that I still had it with my name on it. That gave me the necessary pull up to face the next day with the chipping hammer.

On the run from the Cape to Western Australia, we had fine weather with a good strong westerly wind at all times. It was during this passage that I had the treat of seeing a full rigged sailing ship come up from astern, overtake and pass us as if we were standing still. It was a really fine sight with all sails set and I should imagine every stitch of canvas that the ship possessed. We in the *King Egbert* were doing about 9 to 10 knots, she, the sailing ship, must have been doing about 14 knots.

Port Pirie in Western Australia is a well-known port to nearly all seamen and I am sure that they will have all enjoyed their stay there. For myself, there was the local movie show and whenever we had any free time, we were all ashore with the ship's football. Nearly all the crew were young people who were not interested in the stronger beverages and, after having played football one very hot afternoon, we decided to have a soft drink when returning to the ship. Sighting what we took to be a café, we all trooped in; about ten of us. There were only a couple of tables in the place, one of these being occupied by an elderly couple having tea. There not being enough chairs for us to all sit down, the remainder just parked on the floor around the room, waiting for the waitress or someone else to serve us with some lemonade. The couple who were having tea had stopped and were watching us very intently. Then, when we were all properly settled, the gentleman asked us just what it was we wanted. The order was given for ten bottles of pop. Then we were very sweetly informed that the place we had invaded was no café, but the home of the couple having tea! Imagine the shock they must have had to see ten fellows come in, occupy the remaining table and commandeer all the floor space right in their front parlour. They were very decent about it for we all had a cup of tea before we left and later returned to a party given by the lady and gentleman whose home we had invaded.

Every day, from 7 a.m. to 5 p.m., the deck crowd were employed in painting over the ship's side on stages. My job was the draft figures on the stem and stern and, while painting these from a punt, I was hailed by the bosun to come up on deck as it was 3 p.m., and the afternoon 'smoke-o' of 15 minutes. The ship had just commenced loading bag wheat and she was flying very high out of the water forward. While working my way aft from the bow, I spotted a rope hanging over from the top bulwark rail, tested it to see it was made fast on deck, and then decided to climb up the rope instead of going aft with the paint. Quite a climb or rather should I say a "walk" for I was walking up the ship's side and pulling myself up with my hands at the same time. I got to within arms reach of the bulwark rail when I developed cramp in both arms. I could actually see on the fore-deck, but could not get either arm to take another move upwards.

Nothing else for it but to slide back down the rope into the punt and then continue my journey aft. When I got to the after pilot ladder the 'smoke-o' was over and I was firmly told I'd had it for that day.

Our favourite spot at nighttime was the Felix Café, run by a young lady who had lots of girlfriends. We were very soon friendly with the girl friends too, and arranged a car trip out into the country for the following Sunday. Two cars and all the food we wanted. Some day that was. We enjoyed ourselves without a doubt and I am sure the young ladies did too. Our only difficulty was finding all the party when it came to the time for the return. We had all collected a type of bulrush about 8 feet in height and, with these fastened to the tops of the cars, we made our way back to Port Pirie; arriving there in the early hours of Monday morning. We had nothing to worry about regarding the hour, but the female side of the party had their parents to face and some explaining to do too. That was one night we brave sailors did not want to see them to the front veranda. Those Aussies are all pretty big fellows!

At Monday lunchtime, I was talking about this bulrush affair when the hatch leader from No. 4 hold asked where I had obtained it. When I told him about the trip, his said that one of the girls was his daughter. I can't tell you exactly what he told me, but it was very straight and to the point regarding his daughter and the hour that we had brought her back home. That fellow did not seem to put much trust in the seafaring fraternity.

Owing to the draft of the vessel and the depth of water at Port Pirie, only part cargo could be loaded there. We took half cargo and proceeded to Wallaroo, to complete.

The first night alongside, nearly all hands were ashore to the local dance hall, myself included, hoping to meet some of the local girls without a doubt. In this I was successful and, after a few dances with the same one and then some refreshments, the usual request - could I see her to her home? Sure, but she told me she lived a distance away. What did I care for distance. Before I got back to the ship, I was firmly convinced that the Australian idea of distance and our idea are vastly different. When the dance ended about midnight, I found it required a taxi for this distance. The young lady lived in Kadina, about six miles away. Travelling through the countryside, the driver stopped a couple of times and the young lady had to explain to him that she was talking to me in the back and not to him. Upon arrival in Kadina, the taxi driver told me the fare and I requested that he wait a few minutes to take me back to Wallaroo. But he had been on these trips before and requested that I pay the first fare before he would wait for me to take me back to the ship.

Did he wait? I spent a little time saying goodnight - it seemed to pass very quickly to me at any rate, but I believe time does pass very quickly in Australia under those conditions. When I got back to the road end, there was no taxi, and what a hike back to Wallaroo! As I walked, I wondered what kind of wild life I could meet up with. Were kangaroos dangerous at nighttime?

I made the trip all right, but how I do not know. I had never been on that road before, but found it and got back on board just I time to change into my working clothes and turn-to at 7 am. Was I tired by lunchtime? Still, we had all had a good time!

Sailing day arrived and we had the job of battening down hatches and stowing away winch gear such as blocks and pulleys. We were fully loaded with wheat and our destination was the port of London.

While I was working at the job of taking gear adrift, the Third Mate told me that two young ladies wished to speak to me. The young lady from Kadina had travelled through to say goodbye. I have never set eyes on her from that day, but I have often thought of Miss Ethel White and of the good times we spent together.

"Homeward bound" again, with everyone looking forward to spell at home. For myself, I was hoping that the chances of obtaining a third mate's berth had improved since I was last in England. But no such luck. There were still quite a number of Masters' certificates unemployed, men with years of bridge experience so that my chances of a berth were very slim indeed.

When I arrived in London, I was told by the Chief Officer that, should I wish to do another voyage in the ship, my job was there for me. I took him at his word and, having his permission to go home for a few days leave, set off for Gateshead on Tyne. Everyone who has ever been on leave from a ship will know only too well how quick time flies during that holiday, and I was very soon in receipt of a re-joining telegram.

Before leaving, I decided to pay a visit to the dentist to have two teeth removed two that had been giving me a lot of trouble on the previous voyage. I was met at the door of the dentist's surgery by a very attractive young lady in white. For a moment I thought maybe she was the dentist herself and right there and then I thought "No Gas!", but no such luck. She was the receptionist who showed me into a waiting room, with the usual collection of old periodicals, where I had to wait my turn. She had all the necessary information from me as to the number of teeth (two) to be extracted, then called "next, please". Having convinced myself that I was the only victim waiting his turn — that must mean me. Nice chairs these dentists have, very comfortable. After having my mouth examined, I was informed that I should have them all out owing to the presence of pyorrhoea in the gums. Right-o, carry on with the job. After having been in the chair for about half an hour, the vision in the white coat arrived in the room, to find out who was winning, the dentist or me. When she saw the jar full of teeth that used to belong to me, she asked me why I had said two only. To the best of my ability with a mouth that seemed to me inches out of place, I replied that I had thought so, but the headman had thought different. I had the whole issue of teeth put on the table and what a collection they were. Told by the dentist to return in a couple of weeks time, I had to explain that would be rather difficult as I was leaving that night for London to join a ship bound for China. He wished me the best of luck and I promised to return in about six months, possibly a lot thinner than I was that day.

We signed articles in Poplar Merchant Marine Office and I was very pleased that I got through without having to pass the Federation Doctor, who, I have no doubt, would have stopped my sailing with a mouth like I had. The following day was spent storing ship and then once again we were off, this time for Batum (Batumi), Russia, in the Black Sea, to load a cargo of case petrol for Darien in China.

Proceeding down the English Channel, I had the 6 p.m. to 8 p.m. wheel in the second dog watch. During this time, it was the practice of Captain Poulgrain to come up on the bridge and have a chat with the Chief Officer. While they were standing at the wheelhouse window talking, I was at the wheel going from one foot to another, wishing that it would soon be 8 p.m. and my relief, for my head seemed to be on the point of bursting. And was I hungry too. Just try living in the forecastle, no teeth and on ship's food.. I was practically living on fresh air and the odour from the galley.

Captain Poulgrain turned round very sharp and told me to stand still when I was at the wheel. Then he asked me what course I was steering - SW by S1/2 S - or "Sow West by sow a half Sow", that's what it sounded like. He then asked me what was the matter and upon my telling him he instructed me to report to his room at eight bells!

At last, my relief appeared on the spot and I was very pleased to get away from the wheel and report to the Old Man who examined my mouth, asked me what I had had to eat, then rang for the steward to whom he gave orders for soft food in various forms to be given to me until my mouth had hardened up. This hardening up process was encouraged by my entertaining the remainder of the deck crowd in the mess-room by attempting to consume pickled onions, chasing them all over my mouth from the tonsils to the front door and back again.

My room mate, Jones of Aberavon, was really put out when, at lunch one day, I requested that he should hurry through his meat and veg then get on with the job of chewing mine for me. I would wait! For a while he really thought I meant it!

By the time the ship was made fast in Batum, I could have chewed my way through a horse. The first visit to this country presented quite a shock to me with all its formalities (it still does today in 1950), for, upon arrival, I was sent for to go to the Old Man's room before the port authorities. Presenting myself, I was first asked my name and rank on board. I answered this and then came the question "Did I possess a certificate of competency?" If so, then why was I serving as an AB and not an officer? Captain Pougrain himself tried to explain the position in England that existed regarding employment, but this did not appear to satisfy them and I was informed that I would not be allowed to go ashore during the vessel's stay in Russian waters! I was given the job of night watchman and was pleased when, at the end of two weeks, we were fully loaded with case oil and ready for sea. Then, before leaving, I had again to present myself before the authorities to prove that I was still on board. Little chance I had had to be any other with an armed guard at the foot of the gangway day and night.

Having cleared from Batum for Darien, I was greatly surprised to find the ship heading westerly through the Med and, upon asking the reason, was told that we were going by the Cape. Some run. And in the motor ship there is very seldom any bunkering port enroute. Running to Australia, these motor ships bunkered at Las Palmas when homewards bound and this one bunkering carried them out to Australia then back to Las Palmas the following voyage.

The voyage from the Black Sea to Manchuria was the longest sea passage I ever made, with only one stop en route. We were certainly very fed up with the sight of salt beef and salt pork long before we reached our discharging port. For myself, I promised to have the finest feed of chicken that I had ever had at the first port we touched. This turned out to be Miri in North Borneo to replenish the bunkers. We entered the pilotage waters then down went the anchor. I asked were we waiting for a river pilot to take us to the bunkering berth, but no, this anchorage was the bunkering berth. Picking up the pipeline from a buoy from a shore station, we could just see the distance. I have never seen coal bunkers come on board in this fashion, so we live and learn. At any rate my chicken dinner was delayed for a number of days yet.

At long last we arrived in Darien and immediately upon arrival the ship was invaded by the usual crowd of shore-side salesmen and saleswomen. There were tailors, pimps, rickshaw wallahs, so-so girls and laundrywomen, but most important to the ship's company was the presence of the hairdressers, mostly young boys, and could they do a job of cutting hair! The barber boys had plenty of business that day for we all needed the service of a hairdresser in no small way. We had shears and scissors on the ship and anyone could try their luck with the help of a basin borrowed from the galley.

There was very little tea eaten on board that night at 5 p.m. for everyone was in one mad rush to get ashore to a plate or two of ham and eggs, the sailors' favourite. My watch mate, a young Welshman, Jones from Aberavon, and I were off and into the first café we could find. 7 p.m. found four of us sat around a table at the first decent café we could find and the order given for a double portion for each of us. Did we enjoy that meal! Even without any teeth, I finished in the first three - much to the amusement of the young lady who was waiting on us. Finishing our meal, we ordered a further supply for 11 p.m. Then I inquired of the waitress could I order a large chicken to take back on board ship. I was even then thinking of the following day's dinner (would that I had that appetite today!). Yes, that would be possible, and with everything having been laid on, we left the café to visit the sights of the town.

The port of Darien is quite a large town and there are attractions of every kind under the sun to suit all tastes. During our wandering around, we tried to take in all the sights right away. Dance halls (Russian), cafés, dives and opium dens. And, having visions of knife fights etc., we got away very quickly from the latter. At one café-cum-dive we ran into three of the older deck hands who were really going to town with the local female talent, buying drinks for all and sundry. We joined the party and I attempted to drink or taste one of the so-called wines that the ladies were drinking. Before I was able to do so, the glass was capsized and the "wine" ran all over the table. This stunt is as old as the hills. The ladies of the establishment sit drinking the most expensive drink, but it never has any effect on them for the simple reason that it is only coloured water. Every drink they order brings them so much commission from the management.

After a time, I persuaded the men that they were being gypped and decided to go from there to a dance then back for supper. No difficulty of looking for taxis in this town for wherever the sailor goes, so do the rickshaw wallahs. They merely park on the road outside the café you are visiting and, no matter how long you may be, they will still be there when you come out.

Ever seen the sights of a Far East city? Once seen, they stay with you forever. To do so, Jones and I engaged two rickshaws for, by the time we left the café, there was an army of rickshaw wallahs waiting outside. Jones climbed into one and I into another, then off for the bright lights. The two coolies pulling those rickshaws were out to outdo each other as to speed and endurance. Before long, the steam was rising from the coolie running in front of me. I yelled over to Jones "How are you doing, Jonesie?" "Oh, I'm all right man, but indeed to goodness I think my horse is on its last legs, man!" We travelled from one end of Darien to the other that night, keeping the same coolies and their buggies. What sights! What with beggars, weird music, cafés, shops, and geisha girls serving rice sake. To be sure. there were no local pubs like Fred Woods "the Locomotive" or the "Black and Grey" to see or visit, but look on the other side of the picture, I've not seen any geisha girls in King Street either. I wonder why?

On our return journey to the café we had visited and left the order for the chicken, we met the strangest and funniest sight of the night. Two other ABs, named Ross and McKie (two North Sea chinamen) had been imbibing rather freely and were really out to paint everything a very bright red. Our first warning that they were in the vicinity was the noise and the shouting, Scots, Gaelic and a lot that was possibly Chinese, when around the corner they charged. Ross was pulling one rickshaw and McKie the other, with the coolie wallahs yelling their heads off inside the rickshaws. Ross and McKie were out to show China that the hieland laddies could do anything that anyone else could do, no matter where they lived. The two of them brought a breath of Scotland to Darien that night. I myself could still smell it on them the next morning.

After the dance, Jones and I returned to our café for the feed of ham and eggs, also to collect my chicken. When we had finished supper, I asked the girl for the chicken, to which the reply was, "I go wake him up!" Blimey! What I had ordered was a bird dressed all ready for the oven, here she turns up with a rooster as old as China and making enough noise to waken the whole neighbourhood. What a trip back to the ship in an open rickshaw with that bird. It was one long battle all the way. By the time we got on board, I had more feathers on me that that cock-bird had. I think I won that battle, if not that night, then the next day. I threw the bird in the mess-room for the night, closed the door and went off to my bunk.

Rise and shine sure gets around quick when you are enjoying your bunk. We were called by the watchman who inquired as to what the — had happened to the mess room. He had put the coffee on the only clean spot he could find and I went to investigate. What a shock we got. What a picture that mess room was! That bird must have had a very nervous night and, by the look of that mess room, he had been reduced in size by pounds. When we opened the door, it was the nearest thing I had ever seen to a cattle boat. That bird had left visiting cards from one end of the mess room to the other. I had to clean it all up, but first - the bird! I grabbed him and he was on the receiving end this time.

We had to leave the major operation on our dinner until 8 to 9 a.m. breakfast hour. During that time, Jones and I parted that rooster from his overcoat then came the task of removing the hairs etc. At home I had watched my mother singe a bird over a gas jet, but here on board we had no gas so we decided to put some paper in a bucket, light it and throw the bird in. Did we singe it! We almost cremated it. By the time we had rescued the carcase from the burning papers, it was as black as charcoal with part of the "News of the World" stuck to it.

At 9 a.m. I handed this so-called chicken to the ship's cook, asking him to "cook" it for me. He looked at it and asked me what it was supposed to be and was it safe to eat. He cooked it, we ate it - pullet! We couldn't tear it. I swear that bird must have crowed from every yard as it travelled the Great Wall of China - and me with no teeth!

The discharge of the case-oil was very rapidly completed; there being no shortage of labour out here. Then we were ordered to load a full cargo of soya beans for discharge at Hamburg, Germany. This time via the

Suez Canal and not via the Cape. This cut down our trip home by almost thirty days.

We sailed from Darien fully loaded the week before Christmas 1930. On our trek to Hamburg, New Year's Day saw the change of helm orders put into operation, when we changed our orders of port for starboard and starboard. Up to this time I had always been under the orders that "hard-a-port" meant putting your wheel over to the right, to left for hard-a-starboard. There were quite a few mistakes made during the first few days on both the officers' part as well as the men at the wheel.

Christmas Day, one of the few holidays for the seamen, was spent in the usual way feeding and lazing around during the watch on deck. Then there was the additional tot of rum or whisky and a bottle of beer with your dinner. One day only. The following day came around as ever and another Christmas Day was past and gone.

1931

We arrived in the Bay of Suez one evening in January during the second dog-watch and my trick at the wheel, and were at an anchorage waiting for our search light to be fitted at the bow when I went below at 8 p.m. Four hours below and an easy middle watch to look forward to, but I was mistaken.

At 11.45 p.m. or one bell, I was called by Jones, given a cup of tea and told to go to the wheel at midnight. Oh, no! It was my standby. The Master's ordered that I go to the wheel for, during the first watch, there had been no one at the wheel who could satisfy the Canal pilot with their steering. I was told off to steer from midnight. At 2 a.m., I really smacked that bell four times then waited for my relief - ten past, quarter past, still no relief. I asked the Second Mate would he blow for my relief and he replied, "You are to remain at the wheel until 4 a.m." That really was a long four hours, repeating the orders, "Port a little!" "Steady!" etc. At 4 a.m., I was asleep before I got halfway aft to my bunk and I never moved once I got there until 7.20 a.m., time for breakfast and the order again to return to the wheel. I was sure to get used to this given time.

Four bells (10 a.m.). I looked to the wing of the bridge where the skipper and pilot were conversing. The Captain spotting me, then called the third mate over, "Robinson will remain at the wheel until we are moored in Port Said." That's that! I had spent so many hours at that —— wheel I had almost given up that gnawing for tobacco!

"Make fast fore and aft, that will do the wheel!" Was I pleased to go out over to the main deck and light a cigarette. Later the Chief Officer sent for me and informed me I was off watches for the remainder of the day. We bunkered alongside the oil jetty in Port Said and sailed at 4 p.m. bound for Hamburg. Imagine one of the ABs standing on deck, doing no work and the ship leaving a berth, in those times an event unheard of. At 7.30 p.m. that night Captain Poulgrain sent for me to go to his room He thanked me for having spent so long at the wheel and informed me that he had written to the London Office of the company recommending me for a third mate's berth. He expected a reply upon arrival in Hamburg.

We discharged part of our cargo of beans in Rotterdam, then proceeded to Hamburg with the remainder. While discharging in Hamburg, I was again called amidships to the lower bridge where the master was waiting for me on deck.

"I have a letter here, Robinson, from our London office in reply to my letter from Suez, regarding the prospects of your being employed as third officer. In their reply they state that at the present moment they have no berth to offer, but they ask me to find out what you intend to do upon our return to the UK."

To say this came as a shock is putting it very mildly. Indeed I had visions right away of the bridge of one of the King ships.
"I shall do whatever you consider the right thing to do, Sir," I replied.

"Well, Robinson, my orders are Falmouth for bunkers, then out to Australia again. I suggest you leave the ship in Falmouth for, should a vacancy occur in the near future, there would be very small chance of your getting the berth if you were aboard here on the way to Australia."

Being a single man at the time, on a comfortable ship, good food, good quarters and very little responsibility was a great temptation to stay right there than to face another spell ashore out of work. On the other side, being an AB, even a comfortable one, was not helping me with my sea time for 1st mate, so I made the decision.

"I shall leave in Falmouth, Sir, then await further orders at home!"

So upon arrival in Falmouth, I was the only crew member to be paid off, complete with my railway warrant and the best wishes of Captain Poulgrain. Had I but stayed for one more voyage!

Upon arrival home I re-registered with the MMSA and, back on the waiting list, started watching every postman and telegraph boy anywhere near my home.

Three months passed by in this fashion with no offers from any direction and, as regards shipping, there were more ships being laid up than ever before. Eventually I read in the local paper that the *King Egbert* was discharging in Middlesbrough. I went through to see Captain Poulgrain. He was quite surprised to find me still out of a berth, then he told me the full story.

"You must be having a run of really bad luck, Robinson, for when you left in Falmouth we were all fuelled up for the round trip out and back. I still had to put into the Azores, the reason to land the Third Mate sick with appendicitis, so that we were without a third mate throughout the trip." The Captain then asked me had I heard from the office. I replied that they had no vacancies to offer as yet owing to a number of their own cadets having obtained their second mates' certificates and were waiting for berths.

Owing to the depression lasting such a long time, more ships were tying up every week. And prospects of an officer's berth were very, very slim. Indeed, older men were even now beginning to look for jobs ashore. Some had taken to the door to door salesman method - vacuum cleaners - in fact, almost anything they could turn their hands to.

Two hard cases had quite an idea and that was to go around with a couple of buckets, washing soda and a ladder, picking out the houses that were pained white outside or any light colour, then offer to the owner that they would wash his woodwork back and front for an agreed sum. They made quite a good business out of this idea.

Bill Hay, my co-partner from 1924 to 1929 had a similar idea. He took to washing windows, shop and house. How we laughed later at this recounting of this experience. When he first commenced his window washing business (or should I call it racket), he employed a wee boy to assist him, he at one end of the ladder and Bill at the other, walking about South Shields looking for dirty windows. Knowing Bill, he possibly sent the boy ahead to throw some mud around. Bill told me that, for the first few weeks, he had a struggle to pay the boy's wages out of what he earned. Before Bill quit this business, he had not only boys working for him but a good number of men too.

For myself, I decided to do as other seamen had had to do - take up some work ashore until such time as the depression in shipping lifted and work was obtainable on the bridge of a ship. It was my firm belief that to continue at sea as an AB would result in my remaining an AB for the rest of my life at sea. In the forecastle of any ship, one gets that certain number of hours to work then off duty, any extra time would be paid for in the form of overtime. In addition to this one had, as an AB, practically no responsibility and certainly no night duty nights on board when the vessel was in port. At this time officers had to keep alternate nights on board for which no payment was made.

Owing to the difficulty in obtaining berths as junior officers, there were many shipping companies who, with this lever in their hands, demanded of the officers they employed that they worked additional hours to that of their watches. These were know as "field days": usually two hours of the watch below being spent at some job or other, free, gratis and for nothing, if you hoped to keep your job. A junior officer feeling like raising a kick against this did not need to be reminded of the number of certificates walking about, doing nothing ashore. There were plenty to fill your berth on arrival home.

With this knowledge at the back of my mind, I set out to find work ashore. Seamen ashore are the ideal picture of a fish out of water. Still, after a short while, I obtained an interview with the chief engineer of a large road transport company in the north of England. From the results of this interview, I was started on night duty, 9 p.m. to 7 a.m. as third mate of a bucket and grease gun. I was to wash and grease road vehicles for the wonderful sum of £3.00 per week. Better than being out of work.

For the first few nights, I spent most of my time attempting to find out as to which was the bow and which the stern of some of those trucks. In addition to greasing all the moving parts of the vehicles, I had to see to the oil levels in the gear boxes and differentials, then see to the level of DW in the batteries.

Ever lie under an AEC that was loaded with hides from which dripped water, blood and what have you? I can't recommend this pastime as, in the summer, the fluid is accompanied by large and well-filled maggots and in the winter time you are greeted under the vehicle with large portions of slush come snow that has collected there. All this lying on your back looking upward - boy, keep your mouth shut!

During my work here as night greaser, two of the night staff had to act as night watchmen on Saturday nights, from 6 p.m. to 9 a.m. on Sunday morning. Just my luck, I was selected as one of the night watchmen.

This was a very monotonous job, except for one occasion I remember very well. Around about 11.30 p.m., I was busy selecting a nice comfortable spot, where I could get my head down for a couple of hours, when someone almost shook the doors of the garage adrift. I yelled out "Who is it?" The reply was "Police". I opened the door to their request and in stepped a sergeant. "You the night watchman here?" "Yes, sir!"

"Well, listen to this. Tonight a bank in Westmorland has been broken into, robbed and the manager working late beaten up by three toughs who made off in an MG sports car. Now should these men call here for petrol or oil, ring the police and detain the men until we get here. Understand?"

"Yes, sir. Did you say there were only three of them?"

The police departed and I closed the doors - did I ever close those doors. For the remainder of the night had there been a knock at the front, yours truly would have shot out the back - only three of them!

Sometime later, when I arrived home one morning, there was a letter awaiting me with instructions to attend the office of Milburn and Co, Milburn House, Newcastle, at 11 a.m. Knowing that this might mean a job at sea, I shaved, dressed and ready for action at 9 a.m. I was in the office at the company at 11 a.m. prompt, loaded down with the certificate I had never had the chance of using, and promptly ushered into the inner office where I was asked various questions regarding my time at sea. By 12 noon I left the office, complete with railway warrant and the order to join the S/S *Benwell Tower,* lying in Cardiff, the following day.

Regrettably, George doesn't appear to have written anything between this point and his experiences on the SS Carlton.

(LEFT) GEORGE, AGED 10
(RIGHT) GEORGE, AGED 14

SHEAF SPEAR AT DUNSTON STAITHES

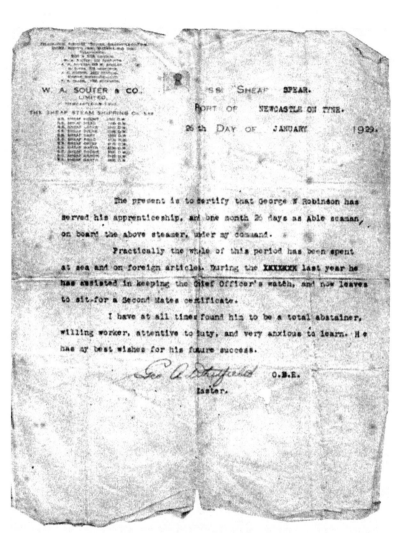

W. A. SOUTER & CO.
LIMITED.

THE SHEAF STEAM SHIPPING CO. LTD

ss. "SHEAF SPEAR.

PORT OF   NEWCASTLE ON TYNE.

26th DAY OF   JANUARY   1929.

The present is to certify that George W Robinson has served his apprenticeship, and one month 26 days as Able seaman, on board the above steamer, under my command.

Practically the whole of this period has been spent at sea and on foreign articles. During the XXXXXXX last year he has assisted in keeping the Chief Officer's watch, and now leaves to sit for a Second Mates certificate.

I have at all times found him to be a total abstainer, willing worker, attentive to duty, and very anxious to learn. He has my best wishes for his future success.

Geo A Whitfield   O.B.E.

Master.

END OF APPRENTICESHIP

Dis. 1.

CERTIFICATE OF DISCHARGE

FOR A SEAMAN DISCHARGED BEFORE A SUPERINTENDENT OR A CONSULAR OFFICER.

ISSUED BY THE BOARD OF TRADE   No 19

Name of Ship and Official Number, Port of Registry and Gross Tonnage.	Horse Power.	Description of Voyage or Employment.
Medjerda 2719 143983 ...ea		PCa

Name of Seaman	Year of Birth	Place of Birth
G. W. Robinson	1910	Gateshead

Rank or Rating.	No. R.N.R. Commission or Conf.	No. of Cert. (if any).
AB		

Date of Engagement.		Copy of Report of Character.
8/8/29		

Date of Discharge.	Place of Discharge.	For Conduct	For General Conduct
4/10/29		VERY B5 GOOD	VERY B5 GOOD

I certify that the above particulars are correct and that the above named Seaman was discharged accordingly.

Dated this ... day of ... 1929   AUTHENTICATED BY

...Sugden...

Signature of Superintendent or Consular Officer.

Signature of Seaman *George William Robinson*

NOTE.—Any person who forges or fraudulently alters any Certificate or Report, or copy of a Report, or who makes use of any Certificate or Report, or copy of a Report which is forged or altered or does not belong to him, shall for each such offence be deemed guilty of a misdemeanour, and may be fined or imprisoned.

N.B.—Should this Certificate come into the possession of any person to whom it does not belong, it should be handed to the Superintendent of the nearest Mercantile Marine Office, or be transmitted to the Registrar-General of Shipping and Seamen, Tower Hill, London, E.1.

MEDJERDA

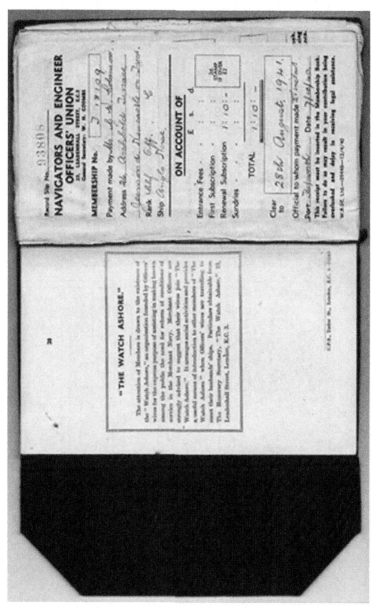

NEOU MEMBERSHIP CARD

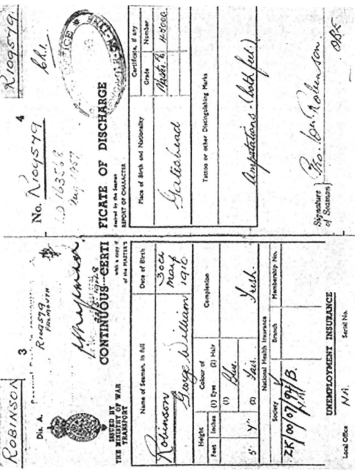

DISCHARGE BOOK

ROBINSON R109579

DISCHARGE BOOK

	CERTIFICATE 5 Or Certified Extract from List and Copy of Report of Character			OF DISCHARGE 6 at Crew and Official Log Book, if desired by the Seaman	Copy of Report of Character	
No.	Name of ship and official number, port of registry	Date and place of Engagement / Discharge	Rating	Description of Voyage	For Ability	For General Conduct
1	Glenwelli Tower 149411.38 Newcastle 157. 2897.	15.3.25 / 1.6.35 Llandaff Myrtle	3rd	Foreign	VERY GOOD 134	VERY GOOD 134
2	Do.	5.7.35 / 16.11.36 North Shields Mate	3rd	Foreign	VERY GOOD 134	VERY GOOD 134
3	Do.	29.11.36 / 29.6.36 Kirk Shields Rowty Mate	3rd	Foreign	VERY GOOD 134	VERY GOOD 134
4	Do.	3.7.36 / 11.11.36 Cardiff Shui Mate	3rd	Foreign	VERY GOOD 134	VERY GOOD 134
5	Dornoch 160053 Glasgow 152.8711	21.11.37 / 11.10.37 Kirk Bryth Mate	2nd	Foreign	VERY GOOD 134	VERY GOOD 134
6	Johncliffe 160013 London 147.2762.	19.10.37 / 15.1.39 Bryth Keth Mate	2nd	Foreign	VERY GOOD 134	VERY GOOD 134

EXTRACTED FROM CREW & LOG

23.5.1948

CERTIFICATE | OF DISCHARGE 8

ROBINSON — 7

Or Certified Extracts from List and Crew of Report of Character

No.	Name of ship and official number, and tonnage	Date and place of		Rating	Description of voyage	Copy of Report of Character		Signature of Master or Officer and of official who makes the entry
		Engagement	Discharge			For ability	For general conduct	
7	Glencliffe 146093 London N.T. 276.1	26.1.38 Keith	30.5.38 South Shields	2nd Mate	H. Foreign	VERY GOOD	VERY GOOD	
8	Grayburn 166670 London N.T. 3735	14.9.38 Island	16.1.40 Victoria Mate Docks	2nd	H. Foreign	VERY GOOD	VERY GOOD	
9	Cadiz 146059 Newcastle N.T. 3205	31.10.40	20.12.40 Liverpool	1st Mate Sea.	Foreign	VERY GOOD	VERY GOOD	
10	Lost Bell 146580 London N.T. 4149	6.11.49	5.5.45 2nd Liverpool Newcastle		H. Foreign	VERY GOOD	VERY GOOD	
11	SHEAF FIELD 162007 NEWCASTLE GR. 2334. N.T. 1075			1st Mate	Hn.	VERY GOOD	VERY GOOD	13 DEC 1940 BLYTH
12	ARROW N.T.1022.		13.1.41 London	1st Mate	Hn.	VERY GOOD	VERY GOOD	MASTER

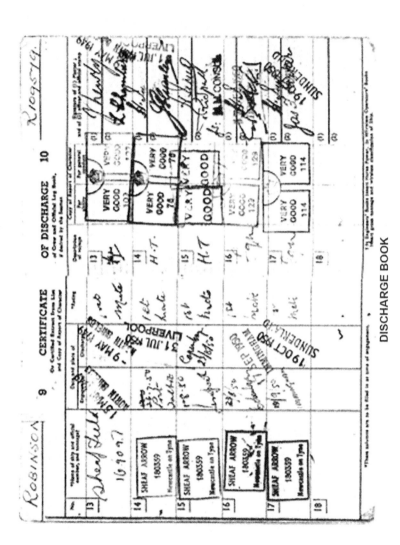

DISCHARGE BOOK

THE MILBURN LINE LTD.,

MILBURN HOUSE,

NEWCASTLE UPON TYNE, 1.

CABLES:
"MILBUS," NEWCASTLE-UPON-TYNE.

S.S. _Bennell Tower_,

Port of _Hull_,

November 4th. 1936.

Testimony of Character.

Mr G.W.Robinson has served in the above vessel as 3rd Officer under my command from I5.3.36 to the present date.

It gives me great pleasure to testify as to his sterling qualities.

At sea he has been in sole charge of the 8 to I2 a.m. and p.m. watches, and during this time I had complete faith in him, being careful in applying the rule of the road regulations and in carrying out the general duties of a watch-keeping officer.

In navigation his work could be relied on.

When loading and discharging cargo, he gave every attention to his duties, having the ship's and Owers' interests at heart at all times.

His sobriety is unquestionable.

To sum up, Mr Robinson has turned out a thoroughly efficient officer, and I heartily recommend him to anyone requiring such.

He leaves us to take his 1st mate's examination.

Master.

Reference

90

GEORGE WHEN SECOND MATE

1940 – CARLTON

SS CARLTON. (Captain W. Learmont). Bound for Buenos Aires from Newport, Mon., sailed in Convoy OB.260 which left Liverpool on 16 December 1940 and dispersed on the 19th. Torpedoed and sunk by the Italian submarine *Pietro Calvi* (Capitano di Corvetta Giuseppe Caridi) on the 20th in position 55°18′N 18°49′W. Twenty-nine died and 4 survived.

The above paragraph gives the bare facts; now here is the grim account given by George Robinson, the ship's 30-year-old 1st Mate.

In that uncertain light between dark and dawn on a cold Atlantic winter morning, I was more than halfway through my watch as Chief Officer of a merchant ship bound south.

We had been in convoy up to noon the previous day, 19th December 1940, then the convoy was dispersed, every ship for itself and Heaven help the hindmost.

Turning from the wheelhouse to walk to the port wind of the bridge I sighted the shape of a submarine close under my port bow, apparently recharging batteries before daylight. I yelled out "Action Stations. Hard-a-port. Submarine." The lookout man sounded the klaxon while I turned the port Hotchkiss machine gun and opened fire upon the conning tower of the sub. By this time we were alongside the sub and the Captain of this ship I was serving on was beside me at the gun. "What is it?" he yelled. (*It may seem strange that Mr Robinson does not name the ship or the Captain, but the War was in progress when he wrote this account and secrecy was paramount.*)

"Submarine now on our port bow, sir." I turned on the gun again and at once we could see the tracer bullets fly into the air from her hull. "By God, it is too," said Captain L. "What nationality?" "I haven't asked him yet," I replied quite truthfully. I had never thought a submarine could crash dive so quickly as that one did! Within seconds we lost sight of her, without having the chance to use our 4" gun aft.

Our next duty was evasive action, 'Full Speed' and every zigzag in the boat, hoping against hope that in the last hour of darkness we could get away from the sub. What a hope, seven knots against twelve and we had the seven.

From that time until 11.30am we ran at full speed, zigzagging, guns crew at station and lookouts posted forward, aft and amidships.

I decided to shave before lunch and had actually lathered my face when six short blasts on the steam whistle – this is it, torpedoes, I ran for the top bridge. When I got to the top of the ladder we were hit amidships, it was raining Welsh coast from our cargo, the ship listed heavily over to starboard. Captain L. turned to me with the order, "Dump the confidential papers, Mr Robinson." This I did by merely dropping them over the side in their weighted canvas bag.

"Books have sunk, sir," I reported. "Very well, we will abandon ship Mr Robinson. "Aye, aye, sir."

I was given these orders by Captain L. as coolly as he would have asked the steward for an extra cup of tea.

The entire ship's company was taken off, half in the starboard lifeboat with Captain L., and the other half in the lifeboat with me. The weather was moderate to fresh, and really cold, the date being 20th December 1940. (When checking the lifeboats before sailing from the UK, Mr Robinson had found them unseaworthy and had had them replaced.)

After a very short conversation with the commander of the submarine who again submerged, I sailed my boat towards the Captain's and brought up a few yards distance. "Any further orders, sir?" I asked.
"Usual thing, out sea anchor and wait for twenty-four hours on the hope that some bright radio op. may have heard our very brief message and the ship might proceed to this position. "Very good, sir," I replied.

Captain L. then shouted, "Good luck, lad. I hope we both make the Pilot Station." "And to you, sir, " I replied. This was the last conversation I had with him. He was by no means a young man. This was to have been his last voyage before retirement. It *was* his last voyage!

In my boat among the men I had an AB named James Patterson. During the short time he had served under me I recognised him as a very capable seaman. He would be about 40 to 45 years of age, and as I was later to find out, very, very tough. Splitting the boat's company into two watches, I took command of one, the 3rd Mate and Patterson in charge of the other.

The boat lying to anchor, head to wind and sea, I told the men to settle down for the night - one watch below, close together and covered, the other around the boat - four hours on, then four hours below.

Before settling down, we opened the bundle of grey service blankets to cover the men. Patterson came aft to me and said, "Oh sir, if you don't mind, can I wet these blankets first?" "Whatever for?" I asked. "They'll soon be wet enough."

"That's right, sir, but a wet blanket will stop the wind cutting through." How right he was, not only in this, but in a great many other things too. I thank God to this day for the fact that Patterson was with me throughout this ordeal, otherwise this would never have been written.

Between dark and dawn of the next day, the weather worsened to a fresh gale. With very heavy seas running, our sea anchor carried away and we had to take to the oars. At daybreak, we were alone. Of the Captain's boat there was no sign. They had gone the first night. From now on, we were on our own – a fight to live in and through some of the worst weather I myself had ever experienced then and since.

Our food supplies consisted of, at the beginning of the trip, some tinned milk, biscuits and a five-gallon cask of water. From the first day, I put everyone on the strictest of rations – one half of a dipper of water twice a day, at daylight and at dark. The rationing of this water was given to Patterson to dole out an equal to every man. He also watched that cask at all times until it was no longer needed. There was nothing left!

Whenever a rainsquall passed over the boat I ordered "Out sail" then we all sat around the side thwarts with the sail between us catching the rain. I can say right now, it takes a lot of rain water to remove the salt from the canvas of the sail.

Again Patterson came out with his ideas, two strands of rope-yarn tied on the spool down the mast, with the loose end at the bottom dipped into a tin also tied to the mast. In this method he supplied us with a lot of drinking water.

The weather was very cold, we were at times washed with green seas breaking over the boat and making bailing practically continuous.

Patterson by this time always relieved me at the sheet and tiller, the 3rd Mate having very wisely given way to a wiser and more experienced man.

Christmas Day arrived and strange to say the weather eased a little, and the sun shone, spirits rose too!

After our morning ration of water, Patterson said, "After this trip, sir, I shall never drink another pint of beer." "Why not, Jock? Going teetotal," I asked. "Och no, sir," said Jock, "I'll have mine in a bucket after this, to make up for what I've missed." "Well Jock, when we get ashore, I shall buy you the largest whisky and the largest beer we can find." How little we knew of the future.

That Christmas Day, although it was the one and only day that we were not struggling to keep the boat right side up, was the turning point of resistance, both mentally and physically.

That night, December 25th 1940, saw the first one of the boat's company to die. I have no intention giving actual names, to do so would be to revive those memories that are best forgotten.

During the night it was reported to me that one of the men was moaning. I had the man laid in the bows under cover to see if anything could be done – there was nothing – he died. As we put the man over the side, I repeated all I could remember or the burial service, I'm afraid it was very little.

In a newspaper clipping, it states that it was a 63-year-old seaman who went mad and jumped overboard after pulling the plug out of the bottom of the boat. While others replaced the plug, Mr Robinson rescued the man who died about an hour later. It also states that, between Christmas Night and New Year's Day, another seven died and were put over the side.

From that day I had the task of keeping the men occupied, pulling at the oars, bailing, singing, even go washing the inside of the boat – any occupation I could think of. The weather was bitterly cold and getting colder, as near as I could estimate as we travelled more to the north westward with drift and leeway than we had sailed south eastwards.

Patterson every day would strip off his boots and socks, then with his wet woollen socks massage his feet, legs, arms and even his feet and chest, saying to me, "Getting nippy now, sir!" I couldn't agree more. What a man, if there was a job to do, he was there. His boyhood had been spent in the Western Isles of Scotland, his ambition at this time was that we would eventually land there with the boat so that he could claim the boat for his for a fishing craft. He certainly worked hard to bring this about.

Day after day, night after night, we sailed and drifted, company getting less each day, burial party every morning.

New Year's day 1941, there was only seven of us remaining as I sat at the tiller and looked around at the men. I wondered if I looked as they did. Eyes sunken in their cheeks, beards, and very little life left. One of these men had recently been rescued by the Royal Navy from one of the German prison ships that attempted to reach Germany. Three of my company were boys 16-17 years of age; boys in years – men in experience of life and death at sea in wartime – seamen – but men! Never a whimper even when dying, maybe an occasional, "Do you think we'll make it, sir? " Is there a man strong enough not to have that thought sometimes? I don't think so.

From the 20th of December 1940 until the 8th of January 1941, we were adrift, travelling where the wind and sea took us. Towards the end of that time, I knew only too well that the watches Patterson took were of much longer duration than those I stood. Upon being relieved by myself, he would cover himself with the blankets, fold his arms across his chest and fall instantly asleep; wakening up as quickly when I tapped his shoulder and said, "Your turn, Jock." "Aye, Aye, sir!"

Then when I lay down he would cover me up, grasp the tiller and the last thing I would see would be his hard stern face watching the Pole Star.

Morning watch, 8th January 1941, with Patterson at the tiller, myself lying down forward, the other remaining men, Pearson and Morris, lying amidships. Suddenly Patterson let out a yell, "There's a ship! Look over to starboard."

I shouted back, "You're mad, there is no ship!" Just then the boat lifted on the wave crest and we could see her, steaming towards us. Never in my life will I be able to put into words the feeling that I had at that moment – RESCUE.

For several days we had not moved much, we did now. Morris and I put out an oar each and started rowing. Pearson tightened up the sail and Patterson steered – where that strength came from I shall never know.

We must have asked Patterson a thousand times, "Can you see her? Has she seen us?" I was trying to row and blow my whistle at the same time. Pearson was waving frantically, Patterson was solidly at the tiller. At last we were around her lee quarter and alongside. SS ANTIOPE – never will I ever forget that name, although she herself was lost next voyage.

The crew on deck threw down lines, we made fast fore and aft, then next came a rope ladder. Like a monkey, Patterson was up that ladder, halfway stopped and returned to the boat. "Och I've got to have a souvenir." He grabbed the drinking dipper and then up that ladder.

The remaining three of us were hauled aboard by the crew who had to do so as we could not make the ladder.

Upon reaching the upper deck, I said to the seaman holding me, "Don't stand me on my feet for God's sake. Carry me. Me feet have given out on me!" I was carried amidships to the saloon, we had at last been rescued.

How many of that ship's company are alive today? I have no means of knowing, but to them all I say, "Thank you", the brotherhood of the sea is stronger than ever. I knew even then that they had all taken upon themselves an additional and greater risk to stop their ship to pick up four survivors. Whilst stopped, she was perfect sitting duck for any u-boat commander.

The Antiope was bombed and sank, in position 53°13′12″N 1°08′18″E, on October 27th, 1941, when on passage from London to New York. One died.
We were landed in Halifax, Nova Scotia, Canada, on 21st January 1941, one month and a day since being torpedoed. We were rushed to hospital; four living skeletons, so the papers wrote – at least we were living!

In an article in the Southampton based Southern Daily Echo, George Robinson said that he and two of his three companions were in a very bad state. Their arms and legs were frozen, their tongues were about four inches thick for want of water, their mouths were "like a furnace", and that he himself had lost 8½ stones in weight.

Three of us were put to bed, but Patterson, still going, had spotted a bathroom. No nurse was going to bathe him – they had quite a job persuading him to get out of that bath.

Three days afterwards, in the evening, there was a knock at my room door. When the nurse opened the door, in walked Patterson, all dressed up in his shipwrecked seaman's outfit – one of everything.

"Good evening, sir, how are you doing?" he greeted me.

"All right, Jock, how are you?" I could even at that distance smell the heather or something Scotch from his breath.

After some of the usual conversation, he said, "Can you get rid of the wee lassie for a while?"

I asked the nurse to leave as my friend had something he wished to speak of privately. Although reluctant, she did so. No sooner was the door closed behind her than – "Remember, sir, all our talk about the biggest whisky and beer when we got ashore?" I laughed and said, "Oh yes, here we are ashore."
"Well," said Jock, "I couldna get any whisky, but I've got some gin. Just open your mouth, sir." From under his coat he produced a bottle of gin – he had fulfilled another promise.

The following evening, Patterson paid another visit, this time to say goodbye. He had joined a ship that morning, having had his fill of life ashore. He was rather peeved during his first day on board his new ship. At the usual lifeboat drill before sailing, he had been told by the boatswain that he (Patterson) appeared to know little about lifeboats. Life's like that.

I have never seen Patterson again since. Through a mutual acquaintance, I have heard that, despite all the Nazis' efforts to stop the Merchant Service, Patterson did not swallow the anchor until 1947. I am also led to believe that he is still attempting to quench the thirst he developed in 1941.

(Signed) Geo. Wm. Robinson OBE LSM
Master Mariner

Due to frostbite, John Morris and George Robinson had both legs amputated below the knees. On his return to the UK, and when he had recovered, Mr Morris became a spot welder in a Birmingham war factory. Mr Robinson, left Halifax in early November 1941, followed by many months in Dunston Hill Hospital in Gateshead. With artificial legs fitted, he wanted to go to sea again, but as the authorities wouldn't allow it, he took a touring job which involved explaining to workers what the Merchant Navy was doing. He did, however, return to sea after the war and commanded his own ship until leaving the sea in 1950. And Isobel Morison, who had nursed him in Halifax, was his wife.

S S CARLTON

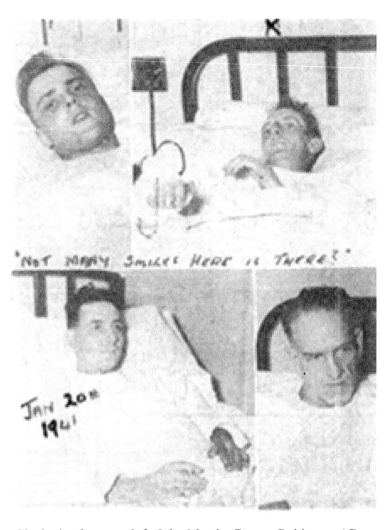

Clockwise from top left. John Morris, George Robinson, AB
Patterson and OS Pearson. Halifax Hospital.

'BADER OF THE M.N.'

Capt. George Robinson, of Gosforth, was awarded the O.B.E. and Lloyds War Medal for "bravery at sea, inspiration and outstanding powers of organisation and seamanship," after the rescue.

Both his legs were amputated, but he went back to sea as a captain— the "Bader of the Merchant Navy."

He spent over two years in hospital and married the Canadian girl who nursed him.

Morris lost both his legs and became an aircraft worker; Pearson, in hospital with frostbite and exposure, went to America.

And Patterson, who complained only of being tired, went back to sea a few days after the rescue ship landed them.

Sunday Sun, Merchant Navy Parade, Newcastle, 1944.

Captain Robinson, with walking stick and standing left of the Lord Mayor, was presented with a sword.

All the information, including photographs and illustrations, was given to me, Ian M. Malcolm, by Captain Robinson's son, also called George. Edited by me and proofread by George's wife, Helen.

Printed in Great Britain
by Amazon